Overlooking the Wy

The lower Wye Valley has been recognised as an area of exceptional landscape quality for hundreds of years. It was here that British tourism was born, with the development of the 'Wye Tour' in the late 18th century. Artists, writers and poets came to marvel at and extol the special landscapes of the Wye, taking guided tours down the river by boat from Ross on Wye to Chepstow, exploring picturesque ruins and specially created viewpoints along the way. By the early 19th century, hotels had sprung up and tour guides besieged the unsuspecting tourists, taking them to the most popular views. The arrival of the railway in 1876 further increased the accessibility and popularity of the area. Today the Wye Valley is one of the best known and most visited landscapes in southern Britain and was designated an Area of Outstanding Natural Beauty (AONB) in 1971.

The landscape of limestone bluffs, gorges and rolling hills clad with ancient forests has for millennia been shaped and moulded by people exploiting the rich mineral resources of the Wye Valley and Forest of Dean. A unique pattern of land use has been created: intricate field patterns interspersed with small settlements, defensive structures, secluded churches, reclusive monasteries, pioneering industrial communities and landscaped viewpoints.

The Cistercian monks recognised both the productive potential and the tranquillity of this landscape when they founded their second abbey in Britain on the banks of the Wye at Tintern. From the late 16th century the character of the valley was affected by intensive industry, as the Wye Valley was one of the earliest places in the UK to industrialise. Fast flowing streams cascading off the surrounding plateau were harnessed to power waterwheels. Iron, copper and

tin works, belc　　　　　　　　　　　　　 vast quantities 　　　　　　　　 ..ᴄ ᴉrom local timber. The Wye made ᴉ easy to import raw materials and export manufactured goods. Quays dotted the riverbank where the associated trades of shipbuilding and boat repairs, rope and sail making developed. River trade waned with the coming of the railway and when the railway declined and eventually closed the Valley's industry died too. The last metal works in the Wye Valley – a tinplate factory at Redbrook – closed in 1961. In 2003 the last industrial site at Lydbrook became a business park. Today's landscape reflects this change. The woodlands, once harvested for charcoal, now stand as continuous and mature forest, often obscuring the views which so delighted the earlier Wye Tourists.

Between 2008 and 2012 the Wye Valley AONB Partnership ran the Overlooking the Wye Landscape Partnership Scheme with £3 million funding from the Heritage Lottery Fund and a wide range of local organisations. Overlooking the Wye embraced a 'string of pearls' – a number of interlinked projects, focusing on helping visitors and local people to understand, enjoy and become involved in the sustainable management of this historic environment. The name 'Overlooking the Wye' relates both to the fact that most of the sites physically overlook the river, and that much of the heritage in the landscape had been forgotten about and culturally overlooked too. This book is intended to help you enjoy the former and overcome the latter, as a legacy for the scheme. You can freely visit most of the places mentioned in this book. We hope you find inspiration in these stories, paintings, poems and photographs which illustrate the remarkable landscape heritage of the Wye Valley.

Front cover: View towards Coldwell Rocks. Main: The Wye from the Eagle's Nest, Wyndcliff. Top left: Enjoying the view at Symonds Yat, c. 1920. Middle left: Overlooking Bigsweir. Bottom Left: The view from Chepstow Castle, c. 1900. Bottom Middle: Wye Woodlands. Bottom right: The *Good Hope* moored at Brockweir 1904. (Neil Parkhouse Collection)

Part 1 **Setting the scene**

Ross on Wye c. 1880. (Monmouth Museum)

Setting the scene

View from The Prospect, Ross on Wye c. 1860.

Tour Boat passing Welsh Bicknor, Nicholas Pocock. (Norwich Castle Museum & Art Gallery) Right: The Reverend John Egerton. (St Mary's Church)

Chepstow Castle. W. H. Bartlett, c. 1845.

Inspirational Valley – birthplace of British tourism

When the Reverend John Egerton began entertaining his guests on the river Wye at Ross, little did he know that he would start a fashion for travel down the Wye Valley that continues to this day. The Wye Tour, a two day boat trip along the Wye from Ross to Chepstow, to view the romantic ruins and picturesque landscape, became the height of fashion in the late 18th century. This was a new type of travel, focusing on the appreciation of scenery, rather than just architecture or history. Tourists came to be inspired by the landscape – to paint, sketch, and write. They followed a set itinerary and dined at specific locations, took walks to famed viewpoints and visited key ruins, making the Wye Tour one of the first package holidays. This was the birthplace of British tourism – and the forerunner of an industry which is now worth £100m a year to the Wye Valley.

Trendsetting Reverend

The trendsetter was the Reverend John Egerton, the Rector of Ross on Wye between 1745 and 1771. He was the son of the Bishop of Hereford, and married to Lady Anne Sophia de Grey. They entertained many visitors and around 1750 he had a boat made specifically to take their guests on river trips along the Wye. Writing some fifty years later the Monmouth printer Charles Heath said that 'the town was continually enlivened by parties of his relatives or acquaintances, which conferred a great advantage on the trading part of his parishioners… whenever any of his friends visited him in the summer an excursion down the Wye formed always a part of their amusement'. Word soon spread about the 'wonders of the Wye' and from this private excursion demand grew for public tour boats.

1

'If you have never navigated the Wye, you have seen nothing.'

William Gilpin, 1783

The Wye near Bigsweir.

The view to New Weir. (Chepstow Museum)

Poets, painters and writers seeking the Picturesque began arriving, helping to stimulate a fledgling tourist industry. Visitors needed places to stay, boats, boatmen and local guides to convey them along the river, as well as provisions for their journey. By the 1770s the trip was a commercial operation, and firmly established as a two-day outing; from Ross to Monmouth on the first day and Monmouth to Chepstow on the second. There was much to inspire the romantic traveller: the scenery, the industry which lined the riverbank, the ruined abbey and castles and the famed Piercefield walks near Chepstow. Some visitors started the tour at Chepstow, some rode rather than taking a boat. William Wordsworth walked. Artists especially, like Turner and Sandby, chose to travel on foot as it gave them time to sketch and paint.

Tintern Abbey, side aisles looking north.
Detail from lithograph by L. Haghe.
(Chepstow Museum)

Popularising the Tour

Chepstow Castle, detail from aquatint by Paul
Sandby, 1775. (Chepstow Museum)

'Tour writing is the very rage of the times', wrote John Byng in 1782. The following year a best-selling guide book, *Observations on the River Wye* was published by the Rev. William Gilpin. He was an artist who, in 1770, paid for a trip down river in a canopy-covered boat, navigated by three men. He wrote *Observations* soon after but delayed publication until 1783, by when a suitable method of reproducing his watercolour illustrations had been found. The development of aquatints, pioneered by Paul Sandby in the 1770s, paved the way for Gilpin to use the technique. This mass production of images brought the beauty of the Wye Valley to a much wider audience than ever before.

Observations was probably the first ever tour guide and it helped inspire what was possibly the world's first package tour. It became the bible for visitors to the area and was soon in its fifth edition. By 1800 the trip had become a must for people of taste and fashion; unable to take the

'...should my pages be the means of imparting any gratifications to the visitors of these delightful regions, I have my first and best reward'

Charles Heath, 1791

Top: Tourists passing trows at Tintern Abbey. Detail from Samuel Ireland's *Picturesque views on the River Wye*, 1797. (Chepstow Museum)
Right: Monmouth printer Charles Heath, 1791. (Monmouth Museum)

A page from *The Wye Tour*, a 'graphic and lucid account of this far-famed stream', by the Rev. T. D. Fosbroke who lived at Ross. (Herefordshire Archive Service)

Grand Tour because of war in Europe they holidayed at home. Monmouth writer Charles Heath cashed in on the popularity of the Tour. He set up a printing business in the town in 1791, producing guides and pamphlets about the Wye Valley which 'have tended to bring into fashionable notice the Tour of the Wye'. As he wrote in *The Excursion down the Wye from Ross to Monmouth* in 1799:

'Whether it be owing to the unsettled state of affairs on the Continent, which renders travelling, if not unsafe, at least disagreeable, – or to that well-founded curiosity, which excites the Man of Observation to survey its attractions, – certain it is that Monmouthshire has, in the course of the last four or five years, been honoured with a very large share of public Notice.'

Many visitors kept journals and diaries as well and by 1850 over twenty guidebooks had been published, firmly establishing the Wye Valley as the birthplace of modern British tourism.

*'The Grouping of this landscape is perfect.
I know of no picture more beautiful.'*

Prince Puckler - Muskau, 1861

View from the Wyndcliff, detail from
engraving. (Chepstow Museum)

Appreciating the Picturesque

New Weir c. 1837 (Monmouth Museum)

**Originally the term 'picturesque' meant, literally, a scene
which would make a picture – as in a painting.** Over time
it came to be used outside the context of art, influencing
garden design, landscape fashions and ornamental walks.
Designers were encouraged to think like artists, especially
when planning enhancements on country estates. One of
these estates in the Wye Valley, Piercefield, became a
highlight of the Wye Tour. Owned and laid out by Valentine
Morris around 1750 it was one of the earliest designed
landscapes in Wales.

Rules for the Picturesque

**William Gilpin was a pioneer in the appreciation of
landscape in Britain and his ideas had a lasting effect
on the way in which we view it.** 'We travel for various
purposes' Gilpin wrote, 'to explore the culture for soils –

5

The Wye near Coldwell Rocks.

Tourists arriving at Goodrich Castle. Detail from an engraving in *The Wye – narrative of a Pedestrian Ramble*, by Leitch Ritchie, 1839.

to view the curiosities of art – to survey the beauties of nature – and to learn the manners of men; their different politics, and modes of life. The following little work proposes a new object of pursuit; that of examining the face of a country by the rules of picturesque beauty.' Gilpin laid down a set of rules defining the picturesque in *Observations on the River Wye*:

'the most perfect river-views are composed of four grand parts: the area, which is the river itself; the two side-screens, which are the opposite banks, and lead the perspective; and the front-screen, which points out the winding of the river... They are varied by...the contrast of the screens...the folding of the sidescreen over each other...the ornaments of the Wye...ground, wood, rocks, and buildings...and colour.'

He recommended that tourists should 'examine the face of a country by the rules of picturesque beauty' – a beauty that was rugged and rough. His rules helped visitors judge the artistic value of a view. Picturesque views were always from a low standpoint, looking upwards to reinforce the feelings of awe and terror which a truly picturesque view should instil. The best way to achieve this was from the low viewpoint of a boat on the river. He named a number of Grand Scenes along the Wye which possessed everything required to be picturesque – according to his principles.

Grand and Beautiful

The first section of the tour from Ross to Monmouth was characterised as Grand and Beautiful; Goodrich Castle and New Weir were Gilpin's Grand Scenes. At New Weir the scenery became more interesting because of the ironworks and industry in the riverside woods where, 'Volumes of thick smoke thrown up at intervals from an iron forge … add double grandeur to the scene.'

Awful and Sublime

The second section of the tour from Monmouth to Chepstow was characterised as Sublime and Awful. Awful in this context meant something which would inspire awe because of its vastness or fearsome grandeur. Sublime was the term used to describe the pleasing experience of this awful beauty. Gilpin thought that Tintern Abbey was 'the most beautiful and picturesque view on the river' and that 'Mr Morris's improvements at Persfield...are...as much worth a traveller's notice, as anything on the banks of the Wye' although he didn't believe that the views were picturesque: 'They are either presented from too high a point, or...they do not fall into such composition as would appear on canvas'.

The concepts of landscape appreciation and conservation have grown out of Gilpin's principles of the picturesque, and his influence continues to this day.

Top: Arriving by tour boat at Tintern Abbey, 1800. Inset: From the letters' page of the Monmouthshire Beacon.

The Windcliff from Piercefield. (Chepstow Museum)

In search of the cynics

Increasing appreciation of Britain's landscapes helped make Gilpin's guide book an instant success, bringing ever more aspiring artists, writers, poets and even royalty to the Wye Valley. But not everyone shared Gilpin's passion for the picturesque. Thomas Rowlandson, one of the leading caricaturists of the time, provided illustrations for a book by William Coombes, which mocked the craze. First appearing in 1809, *Dr Syntax, In Search of the Picturesque* tells the story of a vicar with a hook nose, long chin and a wig who wants to make his fortune by travelling around the country and writing a book about his experiences. And just like *Observations*, *Dr Syntax* was an immediate triumph, capturing the spirit of the picturesque craze.

Looking across the Wye Valley from St Briavels.

Luggage list

· Pens, pencils and
  watercolours
· Pocket edition of
  Cowper's poetry
· Claude glass
· Maps
· Barometer
· Sketch books,
  drawing pads
  and journal
· Provisions for
  a picnic!

Although Gilpin's ideas were ridiculed, visitors continued to follow in his footsteps, as Robert Southey wrote in 1807: 'Within the last thirty years a taste for the picturesque has sprung up; and a course of summer travelling is now looked upon to be…essential…they study the picturesque, a new science for which a new language has been formed, and for which the English have discovered a new sense in themselves.'

Luggage list for the Wye Tour

Travellers in search of the picturesque had some essential items in their luggage, which were necessary to control the untamed landscapes they encountered. Gilpin advocated the use of a Claude glass. This was a small black convex mirror, about four inches wide on a black foil, which miniaturised the reflected scenery. Many artists and tourists used the glasses to manipulate their view of the landscape. This meant they had to stand with their back to the view, looking at it in the mirror! As Gilpin wrote, Picturesque practice always involved some 'improvement' of the landscape. A Claude glass became an essential item in the tourist's luggage.

'In Autumn's forest scenery both painter and poet find here greatest glory.'

Louisa Ann Twamley, 1838

Right: Joshua Cristall's painting of a girl harvesting bracken on Coppett Hill, 1829 – 1831. (© The Garman Ryan Collection, The New Art Gallery Walsall.)

Above: View from Chepstow Castle. (Chepstow Museum) Far right: Cleddon Falls.

Dear Diary...

Part of the enjoyment of travel in the 18th & 19th century was keeping a journal, recording details of what was seen along the way. Many of these diarists simply repeated what Gilpin and Heath had already remarked on! A number were published accompanied with beautiful illustrations. In his *Picturesque views on the River Wye* (1797) Samuel Ireland wrote 'that his drawings should, like the transparent mirror of his stream, truly reflect the landscape that exists around, as well as the objects that decorate its banks.' They offer a wonderful insight into the views which the Wye Tourists of the late 18th century enjoyed.

Ladies of leisure who took the tour kept diaries too, including Louisa Ann Twamley who recorded her journey of 1838 in *An Autumn Ramble by the Wye*. She arrived at Chepstow and travelled upstream, taking a boat to Ross in Monmouth.

Sarah Wilmot wrote about her visit in 1795 when she found that 'bread was too scarce & too dear' for the cottagers at Symonds Yat to buy. Large quantities of corn were exported down the river and Sarah felt 'in this time of general scarcity, it is an evil to be justly complained of'. Sarah also describes how the poor made soap, by cutting ferns 'which they burn to ashes, then wet and mix into paste, then work it in to balls which they then sell for washing and whitening blankets and flannel'. Joshua Crystal, who lived at Whitchurch, painted the fern cutters on the Coppett Hill, who provided the raw materials for this cottage industry.

Despite the fact that picturesque writing often showed a 'disregard of fact in the effort for effect', the observations of tourists such as William Coxe, Sarah Wilmot, Thomas Roscoe, Leitch Ritchie and Mr and Mrs Hall amongst others, illustrate the changes taking place in the Wye Valley during the 18th and 19th centuries.

Artistic appreciation

Inspiring records of the Wye Valley, as viewed through the artist's eyes, were left by many, including J.M.W. Turner, Philip de Loutherbourg and Michael Angelo Rooker. Their paintings and sketch books are now in the collections of our national museums. One of the most prolific was an amateur artist from Hereford, James Wathen, who recorded the Wye Valley between 1790 and 1820. Also known as 'Jemmy Sketch' he sometimes acted as a tour guide and often chose to paint sites which other artists avoided. Cumberland, who visited in the 1780s, felt that 'an artist, possessed of the rare talent of knowing how to chuse, might soon fill his portfolio' if he visited Tintern Abbey.

Poetically picturesque

Poets found inspiration here too. Thomas Gray was one of the first to visit in the summer of 1770: 'The principal… feature of my journey was the River Wye, which I descended in a boat for near forty miles, from Ross to Chepstow. Its banks are a succession of nameless beauties'.

William Wordsworth came in 1793 and in 1798 when he walked with his sister Dorothy from Chepstow to Tintern, and the next day to Monmouth and Goodrich Castle. The waterfall at Cleddon is thought to have inspired *Lines Written a Few Miles Above Tintern Abbey*, in which he recalls, 'no poem of mine was composed under circumstances more pleasant for me to remember than this.'

*Five years have passed; five summers,
with the length
Of five long winters! and again I hear
These waters, rolling from their
mountain-springs
With a soft inland murmur. Once again
Do I behold these steep and lofty cliffs,
That on a wild secluded scene impress
Thoughts of more deep seclusion;
and connect
The landscape with the quiet of the sky.*

William Wordsworth

Robert Bloomfield took the tour with friends in 1807 and published *The Banks of the Wye; A Poem* in 1811. Despite its four volumes its easy rhythm – 'in perfect beauty, perfect ease, the awning trembled in the breeze' – was all the rage! The popularity of the Tour owed much to the printers and publishers who brought these poems and paintings, guidebooks and prints to a wider audience.

'Volumes of thick smoke…add double grandeur to the scene'

William Gilpin, 1783

Blot on the landscape?

The earliest copper smelting furnaces in Britain were established in Redbrook in 1690. This print from 1861 shows the Tinplate Works. (Chepstow Museum)

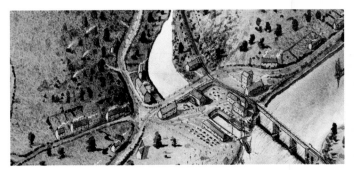

The impact of industry was felt early in Tintern, where a tidal dock was built in 1693. This allowed trows to be loaded with wire from the nearby wireworks, which had been established in 1568.

The now tranquil Wye Valley was one of the earliest areas in Britain to industrialise. Here, the raw materials needed – iron ore, water power and timber to make charcoal – were plentiful. The river allowed raw materials and finished products to be shipped in and out with relative ease. Fast flowing tributaries running into the Wye turned the waterwheels which powered the furnaces, forges, ironworks and wireworks which were at the cutting edge of Britain's industrial development long before the Industrial Revolution.

Far from being viewed as a blot on the landscape the passing tourists loved 'the volumes of thick smoke thrown up at intervals from an iron forge, as its fires receive fresh fuel'. As Gilpin put it, they 'add double grandeur to the scene'.

What happened when...

1568 First Wireworks start at Tintern

1600 Wireworks at Tintern become largest industrial enterprise in Wales

1690s Redbrook is the centre of UK copper production

1700 John Kyrle lays out cliff walk and builds the Prospect at Ross

1745 Rev. John Egerton builds a boat to take visitors down the Wye

1750 Valentine Morris begins landscape improvements at Piercefield

1770 Reverend William Gilpin takes the Wye Tour from Ross to Chepstow

1773 Paul Sandby visits the area with Sir Joseph Banks

1783 Gilpin's *Observations on the River Wye* starts fashion for Picturesque Tourism

1780s David Tanner making cannons at Abbey Tintern Furnace

1789-1815 Restrictions on travel abroad due to French Revolution and Napoleonic Wars

1791 Charles Heath starts printing works and publishing guidebooks

1794 The Round House built on the Kymin by the Monmouth Picnic Club

1797 Samuel Ireland publishes *Picturesque Views on the River Wye*

1798 William Wordsworth writes *Lines composed a few miles above Tintern Abbey*

1801 William Coxe publishes *An Historical Tour in Monmouthshire*

1802 Lord Nelson takes the Wye Tour from Ross to Chepstow

1807 The poet Robert Bloomfield takes the Tour composing *The Banks of the Wye*

1818 Thomas Dudley Fosbrooke publishes *The Wye Tour or Gilpin on the Wye*

1821 20 waterwheels powering industries along the Angidy Valley in Tintern

1820s New roads along the Valley improve access; steam packets arrive from Bristol

1838 Louisa Anne Twamley publishes *An Autumn Ramble on the Wye*

1839 Thomas Roscoe publishes *Wanderings and Excursions in South Wales*

1841 Leitch Ritchie publishes *The Wye and its Associations, A Picturesque Ramble*

1842 William Makepeace Thackeray publishes *Cockney Travels*

Mid C19th Picturesque movement falls out of favour as too restricting

1861 Mr and Mrs Hall publish *The Book of South Wales and the Wye*

1870s Ross to Monmouth and Monmouth to Chepstow railway lines open

1880 1000s arrive by train to watch the moon rise through Tintern Abbey's rose window

1895 Tintern Tinplate Works close

1920s Wye Tour declines after WW1

1938 Forest of Dean designated as the first national forest park

1949 Redbrook Tinplate Works producing 43,500 boxes of tinplate weekly

1961 Redbrook Tinplate Works close

1971 Wye Valley designated as an Area of Outstanding Natural Beauty (AONB)

Anne Rushout painted the scene at New Weir in 1802. (Chepstow Museum)

Commodious conveyances

Wye Tourists afloat at Lydbrook, c. 1880.
(Dean Heritage Museum Trust)

Think of the Wye as a watery highway linking the riverside villages with the wider world and you'll begin to understand its importance in earlier times. The Wye had been a shipping route for hundreds of years and was the main trade route between Hereford, Chepstow and Bristol. Boatmen navigated flat-bottomed, white-sailed river boats called trows, which carried everything from hops and herrings to cider and coal.

As the fashion for picturesque travel grew, boatmen who knew their local history (or at least could tell a good story) saw an opportunity. They built their own tour boats. Like a trow they could be used with or without a sail and had a mast which could be hinged down to fit under bridges. Most had a covered canopy to protect passengers from the sun or rain. Cushioned seats were arranged around a table so passengers could sketch or write during the voyage – a 'floating parlour – a most commodious conveyance', wrote

Detail from an engraving by Robert Havell published in 1826, showing a tour boat at Chepstow. (Chepstow Museum)

This photograph from the 1880s shows a Wye Tour boat, without its canopy, moored at Symonds Yat. Many tourists compared them to Venetian gondolas. (Neil Parkhouse Collection)

one of the passengers in the 1830s. Louisa Ann Twamley said that the boat she took 'looked as if it wished to be taken for a gondola's fifteenth cousin'!

Some guides advised the tourists to keep well out of earshot of the boatmen so 'the ear is not pained by the coarseness of language heard too frequently from the navigators of public rivers'! Usually there was a crew of three, one to steer and two to row. Sometimes the tourists had to get out and walk as the boats had to be hauled over the shallows by the crew. As Joseph Farrington wrote in 1803, 'the pleasure we had in viewing the scenery was frequently interrupted by the difficulty of getting our Boat over passages so shallow that it seemed almost impossible to force it forward. It was frequently obliged to be lifted with poles by the men standing in the water'.

Taking the Tour was not cheap, the equivalent of several hundred pounds today. Joseph Farrington reported that the cost between Ross and Monmouth was 'one guinea and a half for the boat, and half a guinea to the Boatman…It is also usual to take a basket of provisions from Ross to eat in the boat at such a place on the passage as may be preferred.' Despite the shallows and the cost tour boats became a common sight all along the river and could be hired throughout the summer months, as The Halls noted when they took the Tour in 1861:

'Excellent boats, well and carefully maintained are to be obtained either at Hereford, Ross, or Monmouth: the charges are somewhat high, necessarily so, considering the heavy labour attendant on the return. For a boat with one man, the charge from Ross to Monmouth is 15s., the distance being twenty-three miles; for a larger boat, with two men the charge is 30s. When the lighter boat is used, the boat man finds it easier to bring it back by land, on a truck, the distance only being 10 miles; when the heavier boat makes the voyage the men are compelled to draw it along the shore, the difficulty of rowing up stream being (as we have intimated) very great, in consequence of the extreme rapidity of the current.'

The heyday of the Wye Tour was between 1770 and 1830, but it remained popular well into the steam age. The arrival of the first steam packet boats in Chepstow in 1822 opened up the Wye Valley to the residents of Bristol and beyond. Soon the packet day trippers alighting in Chepstow outnumbered those who arrived by tour boat from Ross.

Sunday best for the photographer at Lydbrook,
c. 1895. (Neil Parkhouse Collection)

Pleasure boats and paddles

Pleasure boats at Symonds Yat.

The opening of railway stations at Ross and Symonds Yat enabled ever more visitors to appreciate the wonders of the Wye. 'Pleasure boating' became the new fashion on the river and as the number of boats for hire increased bye-laws were brought in to regulate activities and to set prices. At Symonds Yat alone there were at least 25 boatmen plying their trade by the early 20th century. With so much competition they handed out little cards promoting their excursions to passengers alighting from trains. This was probably one way of getting around the local bye-laws which forbade the boatmen from 'calling out or otherwise to the annoyance of any person'!

Boats for hire at Monmouth, c. 1900. (Monmouth Museum)

Canoes at Symonds Yat.

A sculler on the Wye at Monmouth.

Peter Gordon Lawrence, founder of PGL. (PGL)

The Ward Lock guide to The Wye Valley, published in 1925, offered some practical hints for boating on the Wye and recommended that 'Should ladies be in the boat, it lessens the risk and lightens the craft to land them on approaching a weir, when they can walk along the bank and rejoin the boat in smooth water'. After World War II motor boats began to replace rowing boats, although they couldn't go downstream over the rapids. In the 1970s the first waterbus from Amsterdam arrived.

A new kind of tour began in the 1950s when Peter Gordon Lawrence started leading canoe trips down the Wye, camping overnight on the riverbank. His company, PGL Voyages, has become one of the leading travel and outdoor youth adventure companies in the country. Canoes and kayaks now navigate in place of tour boats and trows. But a trip down the Wye remains as popular and inspiring as it did 250 years ago.

'This scene is greatly enlivened by the passing of vessels up and down the river; – if the wind sets in up the current, a number following each other under different sails, give it an interesting as well as picturesque appearance.'

Charles Heath, 1808

A trow near Ross. Samuel Ireland, 1797. (Chepstow Museum)

Water fights and navigation rights

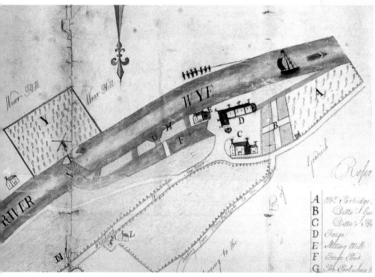

This map of New Weir ironworks in 1758 shows seven bow hauliers pulling a trow towards the lock. Water was diverted to the right to power the ironworks. (Monmouth Museum)

Boats sailing up and down the Wye may have added to the picturesque scene for the tourists, but they were absolutely vital to the livelihood of people living beside the river. There was no riverside road between Chepstow and Monmouth until 1828 so the Wye was the focus of travel and trade. Boat trips for the tourists were only possible because of the navigation rights which had been established by Edward I in the late 13th century. These privileges recognised the importance of trade on the Wye, which in the Middle Ages had been known as the King's High Stream. This right to navigation meant there was free passage for 120 miles below Hay on Wye.

In reality there were many obstructions and frequent clashes between those who wanted an easy trade route, and those who wanted to build weirs to improve fishing or divert the flow to power the burgeoning industries along the river. As early as 1301 a commission looked at 'the weirs, dykes and stakes in the water of Wye between Hereford and Monmouth, as it appears that boats cannot pass as they were wont'. In the 1330s Henry of Lancaster

A trow navigating the lock at New Weir.
(Monmouth Museum)

'We have prepared some Bills for making small Rivers navigable...it easeth the People of the great Charge of Land Carriage; preserves the Highways, which are daily worn out with Waggons carrying excessive burden; it breeds up a Nursery of Seamen.'

Sandys' scheme was unsuccessful, although an Act of 1695 did remove all the obstructions apart from New Weir. However, taking the weirs away quickened the flow of the river with the result that it was often too shallow. In 1763 Isaac Taylor surveyed the river, drawing up a scheme to build twenty-two weirs, with locks, between Bigsweir and Hereford. This would enable barges of thirty or forty tons to be pulled by five or six men. Costing over £20,000 the scheme was not implemented.

At the only remaining weir, which fed the New Weir ironworks, the owner had to provide a lock for boats to pass. Taylor's survey of 1763 pointed out the danger here, where 'the water from the Lock and that from the Salmon Wear meeting forms an eddy below the Lock, into which if a barge falls she is in danger (if deep loaded), and many have been sunk; it is always with difficulty they are drawn out'. This weir was finally taken down in 1814, following the closure of the ironworks. With obstructions removed trade along the Wye-side wharves flourished, even though navigation was 'altogether dependent on the state of the seasons, being equally incommoded by floods in winter and want of water in summer'.

complained that 'boats and ships with wines and victuals and other lading could not cross to the earl's town of Monmouth.' This was because the abbot at Tintern Abbey had raised the weir there by six feet to protect his salmon supply!

In 1640 a Grand Jury in Hereford found that 'weirs on the Wye were a nuisance and a hindrance to navigation', but early attempts to remove these obstructions met with fierce opposition from the highest levels: in the 1660s the newly formed Navigation Trust was ordered not to meddle with the weirs held by the King.

Sir William Sandys, a pioneer of river navigation, was the first to try and establish the Wye as a commercial waterway in the 17th century. The incentive to improve navigation came from the flourishing metal industries at Lydbrook, New Weir, Redbrook, Whitebrook and Tintern. This area along the Wye and into the Forest of Dean was of national importance, for it was here that new metal making technologies were being developed and adopted. In 1577 two tons of iron had been brought from San Sebastian in Spain on board the 30 ton *Elizabet of Chepstowe* to the new wireworks at Tintern. In 1697 1000 tons of copper ore were shipped from Cornwall through Chepstow to the centre of UK copper production which at this time was Redbrook. And as exports of finished iron, wire, copper, timber and oak bark grew so the need for easy navigation became more important. As a Bill to the House of Lords in 1665 read:

Navigation rights

An Act for making Navigable the Rivers of *Wye* and *Lugg* in the County of *Hereford*.

Whereas the free and open Navigation upon the Rivers Wye and Lugg, and the Streams falling into them may be a great Increase of Publick Trade, and a beneficial easie conveyance of Ship-Timber, and a continual Nursery of Seamen for the Supply and Service of his Majesties Navy.

Fig. 2 Part of the preamble to the Wye Navigation Act 1695

One hundred miles of free navigation rights still exist on the Wye, from below Hay on Wye, down to Bigsweir and into the tidal waters, one of a very few rivers in the UK where these traditional rights remain. From time to time boats manage to navigate far inland: in 1989 a 150 foot, 230 ton motor barge, the *Wye Invader* reached Hereford , returning downstream in the winter of 2012-2013. (Herefordshire Archive Service)

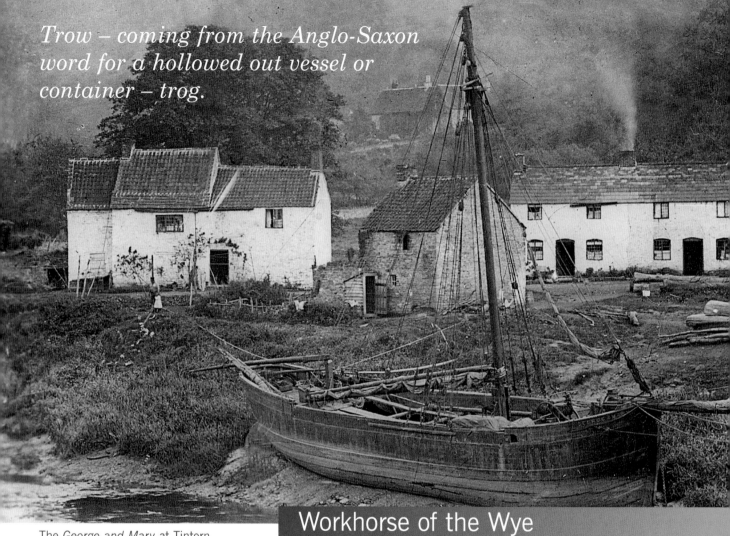

Trow – coming from the Anglo-Saxon word for a hollowed out vessel or container – trog.

The *George and Mary* at Tintern, c. 1890. (Graham Farr Collection, courtesy of Friends of Purton)

Workhorse of the Wye

The boats working the Wye were called trows. They were simple cargo boats with an open hull which were well adapted to the shallow waters of the river. They had a single square sail which could be used when winds were favourable and a mast which could be lowered to pass under low bridges. With a flat bottom a trow could sit on mud-flats and riverbanks to be loaded and unloaded regardless of the tide or the amount of water in the river.

A laden trow passing Tintern Abbey.

A clinker trow like this one moored at Monmouth would have been able to carry about 30 tons. The white paint at the bow was to make the trows easier to see in the dark. (Monmouth Museum)

A rare photograph showing a trow with sails unfurled at Llandogo, c. 1905. (Neil Parkhouse Collection)

The trow became the workhorse of the Wye, carrying 'large quantities of cider, grain and oak bark down the river to Bristol and other places', as Piggots' directory for 1830 states, 'and by means of the same navigation the city is supplied with coals from the Forest of Dean'. Throughout the 18th and 19th centuries there were regular market trows from Hereford, Ross, Monmouth, Brockweir and Chepstow crossing the open waters of the Severn to reach Bristol.

The account books of the Hereford trow *Charles* show it carried chests of soap, bundles of hemp, barrels of pitch, cider, vinegar, sugar, tobacco, bags of coffee, cases of wine, anchors and a clock-case during the 1820s.

On a good spring tide fifty ton trows could reach Llandogo, just below the tidal limit of the Wye at Bigsweir, some twelve miles inland. Brockweir was the highest the largest trows could reach assisted by the tide. Here cargoes were transferred to smaller, lighter trows and barges which could negotiate the shallower water upriver. The bigger trows developed their sea-going ability to transport bark, ores and finished iron products as far away as Cornwall, Cumbria and Ireland. They became more like a sailing ship with several sails, a deck and a closed cargo hold. As Gilpin wrote, 'little barks lay moored, taking in ore and other commodities from the mountains. These vessels, designed plainly for rougher water than they at present encountered, shewed us, without any geographical knowledge, that we approached the sea.'

Pirates on the Wye?

The notorious 16th century pirate John Callice was born in Tintern and piracy on the Wye was not unknown. Records from the late 18th century, at a time when corn was being exported whilst local people went hungry, show that barges were boarded at Lydbrook by local men and women. At Joyford wheat and flour was taken from a barge and in 1800 at Redbrook a cargo of wheat and flour was seized by local people and sold.

'Now and then, a boat with oars or sail, or a laden barge, passes up or down, the boatman's song ascending.'

Watermen of the Wye

Sailing a trow was a skilled job, especially because the river was often in flood. Although dangerous, flooding helped the trows and barges reach further upriver. Not enough water caused disruption as Samuel Ireland found in 1797, 'This being a remarkable dry season, barges have been laying at Hereford for upwards of four months, for want of water to carry them down.'

Even when river levels were normal it was often impossible to sail against the current so gangs of men called 'bow hauliers' dragged the boats upriver. Fifteen men were needed to take a twenty-five ton trow from Brockweir to Monmouth. 'How they are bathed in sweat and rain', wrote Reverend John Fletcher in 1827. 'Fastened to their lines as horses to their traces…If there is any difference it consists of this: horses are indulged with a collar to save their breasts.'

An 1810 *Prospectus for establishing a Horse Towing Path* made a clear distinction between the 'Watermen who are navigators of the trows and barges, and live on the water, and Bowhallers who drag them against the stream; the latter are unacquainted with the management of the vessels, and only officiate in the servile capacity of Horses'.

It was the custom in Monmouth to give a man a pint of ale, called a mugging, when he was hired. Charles Heath records that if the bargain wasn't kept, the hired man faced three months in gaol (a serious mugging). He provides a vivid description of the bowhauliers at work:

William Pick from Pen y fan, one of the last trowmen, beside his trow at St Briavels' Wharf c. 1885. (Neil Parkhouse Collection)

Trows loading limestone at Lancaut early 20th century. (Chepstow Museum)

'In passing the different weirs they are then obliged to fall, with force, flat on the ground, which is done by the shout of yo, ho! In which position they lie for a short space, when on another shout being given, they rise up, and ….so on…' Men were still being used as 'horses' even after a horse towpath was constructed in 1811.

Rope marks cut into the soft red sandstone of Wilton Bridge are a poignant reminder of the men whose strength pulled the boats up river. In some places capstans and pulleys were needed to assist the hauliers. A plan of New Weir drawn in 1758 shows a capstan used to haul the boats into the lock. In Monmouth there was an especially strong rapid just below the bridge, so a pulley was fixed to the bridge to assist the barges through the current. This must have been an old problem as a survey of the river in 1697 described how 'those that have occassion to go higher up the River Draw their Boats 100 yards by the end of the bridge with Oxen or Horses'.

Where the towpath passed from one side of the river to the other it was called a roving. This happened where the cliffs were too close to the bank for the bow hauliers to be able to pull their barges through. There were at least eight rovings between Monmouth and Ross, using bridges and ferries.

In 1808 an Act of Parliament was passed establishing a horse towing path between Hereford and Lydbrook. When it opened in 1811 horses largely replaced men, although some records show that men were still being used as bow hauliers as late as the 1860s. This was because the Act stated that 'Vessels may be hauled by men only without being subject to tolls'!

In the 1820s experiments began in 'the application of steam vessels to towing barges &c. along canals and rivers'. In January 1828 the Bristol Gazette reported:

'A vessel for such purpose and also for the conveyance of passengers and light luggage has lately been launched on the river Wye at Hereford… no fears are entertained about its utility except in summer season when the shallowness of the river may not afford sufficient depth for the working of the paddles.' The shallows probably won, as trows remained the boat of choice on the Wye.

Trade on the river between Ross and Hereford began to decline when the Hereford to Gloucester Canal opened in 1845. Trows couldn't compete with the railway which arrived first at Ross in 1855, at Symonds Yat in 1873 and stations between Monmouth and Chepstow in 1876. By the end of the 19th century the inland river trow had disappeared. Some trow men adapted their boats to cope with the treacherous open waters of the Severn Estuary and a few trows, fitted with engines, continued to work the lowest reaches of the river in the 20th century, carrying limestone from the quarries below Tintern.

All aboard for a tour down the Wye ...

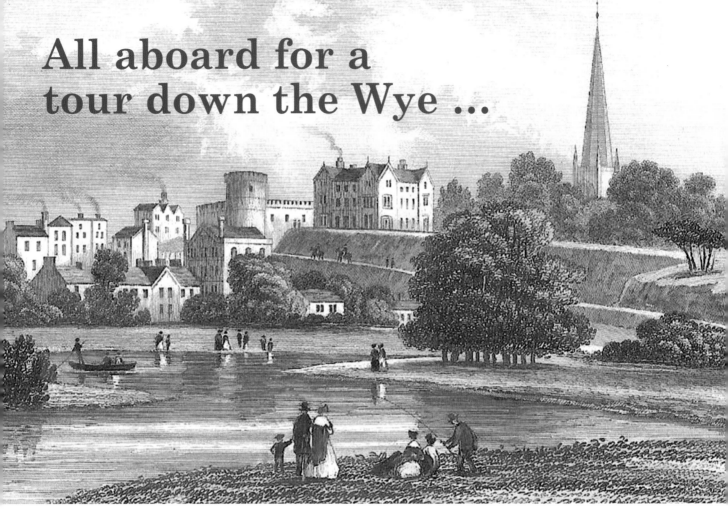

Tourists at Ross in the 1830s.

Boats for hire at Henry Dowell & Son, Ross c. 1905. (Neil Parkhouse Collection)

'The peculiarities of this river, attracting so many travellers have taught the people of Ross to provide pleasure boats for their accommodation. They are built to hold ten persons commodiously, have an awning to shelter from rain or sun; a table to draw or regale upon; lockers to hold books, or bottles and benches for four or five men to navigate the boat.'

Sarah Wilmot, 1795

Ross on Wye
A picturesque prospect

The tradition of catering for visitors began some years before Ross became the starting point for the Wye Tour.
Around 1700 John Kyrle laid out public gardens and walkways on the cliff top beside St Mary's churchyard, which he donated to the town. Commanding views over the Wye, this pleasure ground known as The Prospect had been delighting visitors for some fifty years before the Reverend Egerton began entertaining his guests on the Wye. Charles Heath writing in *Excursion down the Wye* in 1791 described how, 'at the extremity of the walk is placed a Summer House which affords an agreeable retreat, as well as a pleasing view of the river and country'.

All aboard the *Wilton Castle* c. 1906. Can you spot the man with a pole to punt the steamer out of difficulties if it ran onto a shoal? (Neil Parkhouse Collection)

Detail showing tourists embarking on the Wye Tour at Ross Dock c. 1820. (Herefordshire Archive Service)

All Aboard

The riverside below The Prospect became the starting point for visitors embarking on the Wye Tour. The area in front of the Hope and Anchor had traditionally been the town dock and it was here that the tourists hired boats fitted with 'every suitable convenience' and reassuringly supplied with boatmen 'well skilled in navigation'!

When Thomas Martyn took the tour in 1801 George Evans was the steersman of his boat and the oldest waterman on the river. George had been one of the first men to captain the Reverend Egerton's boat in the 1750s and as a result was known as Commodore Evans. He ran two of the regular pleasure boats provided for tourists – the *Friendship* and the *Prince of Denmark* (apparently named after a passenger). Mr Evans helped visitors arrange their journey, advising on provisions and carrying tourists' luggage down to the boats.

At least eight boats were operating from Ross by the time the *Paul Pry*, a steam boat offering trips on the Wye, was launched in 1827. Another steam boat *The Man of Ross*, was running day trips between Ross and Chepstow for 10 shillings in 1836. 'Pleasure boats to all parts of the River Wye conducted by experienced and careful Boatmen' were still being advertised in the 1890s. One Ross boatman, Joseph Evans, was said to have made more than 1200 trips down the river over his forty year career.

In the early 20th century visitors could hire rowing boats at the Hope and Anchor and at Dowell & Son's premises next door. Dowell offered trips to Monmouth stopping at Goodrich Castle, Lydbrook for lunch, Symonds Yat, and arriving by 5pm in Monmouth. Henry Dowell built boats, including the *Wilton Castle*, which was a steam launch with seating for 100 passengers (but only 45 lifebelts), launched in 1902. Its funnel could be lowered to negotiate under Wilton Bridge. Excursions on the *Castle* lasted until the outbreak of World War I, after which the boat was left to rot away on the riverbank. The metal rings where tour boats once moored are still visible on the riverside steps beside the Hope and Anchor.

Wilton
A good trade on the river Wye

'A good trade on the river Wye' at Ross had been noted by Daniel Defoe in the 1720s. Wharves were situated either side of Wilton Bridge, which Charles Heath wrote 'might properly be called the quay or wharf to Ross, by furnishing a convenient accommodation for the shipping and landing of goods sent up and down the river'. Although far inland, the river linked Wilton with the wider world; it was easier to get to Bristol by boat than reach nearby towns along the rutted roads.

Warehouses lined the river either side of Wilton Bridge as well as inns catering for the travelling tradesmen and watermen using the river. River traffic was the lifeblood of Wilton until the railway arrived in 1855, killing off trade.

A trow at Wilton Castle, 1797 from Samuel Ireland's *Pictureque Views*. (Chepstow Museum)

Fords and ferries

Goodrich
Gilpin's first grand scene

Goodrich Castle was the first Grand Scene on the Tour where the view was 'correctly picturesque', according to Gilpin. 'We rested on our oars to examine it', wrote Gilpin. 'A reach of the river, forming a noble bay, is spread before the eye. The bank, on the right, is steep, and covered with wood; beyond which a bold promontory shoots out, crowned with a castle, rising among the trees.' The Castle was built to guard a ford across the river on one of the main Roman roads into Wales. This place was later known as Goodrich Boat or Goodrich Rope where a horse ferry crossed the Wye. Tourists wanting to visit the Castle landed at the ferry house to walk up to the ruins, which Clark's 1866 Guide to Monmouth described as 'frowning from a bold promontory on the right'!

In 1800 there were at least twenty-five ferries between Ross and Chepstow. These ferries linked the communities living on either side of the river, enabling foot passengers, cargoes and animals to cross the Wye. 'The Ferry-boat is guided by a rope' wrote Reverend Fosbroke in 1818, 'a custom certainly of the fourteenth century, and probably of the earliest date in narrow rivers.' Most were hand powered where the ferryman pulled the ferry to the other bank, using a cable which crossed the river overhead. The only surviving traditional hand pull ferry still working regularly on the Wye is at the Saracen's Head at Symonds Yat East, where it saves a five mile trip by road to reach the other side. Mules carrying fuel to the furnaces on the Great Doward were regular passengers on this ferry in the 19th century. Their 'unerring sureness of foot' as they stepped into the ferry boat 'with sagacious staidness' was noticed by the tourists!

Many ferries ran from riverside pubs and at Symonds Yat West there was a second ferry at the Ferrie Inn. There were two ferries in Redbrook, one running from the Boat Inn (boat being the name given to a ferry in Herefordshire), whilst the Upper Ferry ran closer to Monmouth.

At Lydbrook the ferry was a punt-like boat which was poled across the river diagonally. At Brockweir the ferry was poled in the shallow water to start it off and then sculled across the deeper water with one oar, which was placed in a groove at the stern of the boat. The current could be extremely strong here when the tide was flowing rapidly so the ferryman needed to pole upstream along the bank to compensate for the current which carried the boat downstream as they crossed.

Top: Goodrich Castle.   Above: Detail from Samuel Ireland's *Picturesque Views* showing the Goodrich horse ferry. (Chepstow Museum)

Ancient hand ferry at Symonds Yat. (Monmouth Museum)

'... this sooty commerce'

Samuel Ireland, 1797

The Lydbrook Valley in the 1950s.
(Neil Parkhouse Collection)

The view from above the viaduct, 1870s.
(Ian Pope Collection)

Lydbrook
A sooty commerce – where river, road and rail meet

Lydbrook was the first industrial village the tourists passed. This was no sleepy, forest village, but an industrial hub where river, road and later railway, met. Industry started here in 1608 with a blast furnace and forge powered by the brook running into the Wye. The nearby coal mines looked to Lydbrook as the closest point on the river through which to export coal, as William Coxe noted in 1801: 'From Lidbrook large quantities of coal are sent to Ross and Hereford; and we passed several barges towed by ten or eleven men, which by great exertions are drawn to Hereford in two days.'

Lower Lydbrook c. 1895. The tinplate works were just to the right of the pond. (Neil Parkhouse Collection)

Donkey deliveries around Lydbrook c. 1910. (Neil Parkhouse Collection)

In the 20th century a big cable-manufacturing works flourished at nearby Stowfield. These munitions workers were just a few of the 650 employed during WW1. They produced 15,000 miles of cable for field telephones used on the western front. (Lydbrook Historical Society)

Conditions were punishing at Lydbrook's tinplate works, a 24 hour operation carried on through the night by the light of tar lamps. (Lydbrook Historical Society)

Industry boomed to such an extent that tourists floating past on the river in 1861 wrote, 'We may, for the moment, fancy ourselves gazing up one of the wooded slopes that border the busy town of Sheffield'. At its peak Lydbrook boasted seven iron manufacturing sites, a tinplating works and wireworks.

Donkeys were used to carry coal and deliver domestic goods like bread, but as industrial production boomed local entrepreneurs looked for an easier way to move their products, especially coal, around. In 1803 the first tramroad reached the Wye at Lydbrook; Mr Teague's railway began high in the Forest near Mile End, at Teague's Deep Engine Pit. In 1809 another 'railed way' arrived, the Severn & Wye, which originated at Lydney. This tramroad along which a horse could pull up to 12 wagons at a time, brought coal, stone and metal products from the Forest to the hilltop above the Courtfield Arms. From there a steep incline reached down to the riverside wharves.

In the 1870s, a more sophisticated railway arrived, the Severn & Wye & Severn Bridge Railway, which required the construction of a massive viaduct. Building began in 1873, with wooden scaffolding inching out across the valley until the enormous structure, ninety feet above the ground, loomed over the village. The first goods were transported over it in 1874 and the first passengers were carried in 1875. However this giant astride Lydbrook, whose shadow fell across the valley daily, lasted for less than a century. The railway closed in 1956 and in 1965 cranes arrived to dismantle the viaduct.

The Wye gorge at Symonds Yat.

Symonds Yat view. (Chepstow Museum)

Symonds Yat Rock
A view of great grandeur

Soon after Lydbrook the towering cliffs of Coldwell Rocks came into view. Many tourists alighted from their boats here for the ascent to Symonds Yat. Thomas Roscoe made his 'weary way to the summit, through a wood abounding in curious plants' where 'a view of great grandeur displayed itself, and reclining on the turf, telescope in hand, I quietly enjoyed it'. This was William Gilpin's second grand scene on the Wye:

'The river is wider than usual in this part, and takes a sweep round a towering promontory of rock, which forms the side screen on the left, and is the grand feature of the view. On the right side of the river the bank forms a woody amphitheatre, following the course of the stream round the promontory: its lower skirts are adorned with a hamlet, in the midst of which volumes of thick smoke thrown up at intervals from an iron forge, as its fires receive fresh fuel, add double grandeur to the scene.'

This cliff top location attracted much earlier people too. Visitors walking from the Forestry Commission car park to Yat Rock today pass through the ancient ramparts of an Iron Age hillfort, but just as John Maclean noted in 1880, 'Of the thousands of persons who annually visit and admire the diversified scenery from the top of the rock, very few indeed are conscious that they are standing within a fortification of very considerable strength, which at some very early date was held by our British Ancestors against invading foes'.

Edwardian visitors enjoying the view. 'Nothing should tempt the tourist to give up the water', wrote J. A. Stratford in 1896, 'because the charm of the river scenery cannot be fully witnessed from the land, or sufficiently realised during the speedy transit of a railway journey.'

A Wye Tour boat below Coldwell Rocks, where The Halls landed in 1861, 'to walk up and down hill for about a mile; the boat meanwhile makes a voyage of five miles, and rejoins us, giving us time to ascend Symonds Yat...and hence you have a view in seven counties.' (Chepstow Museum)

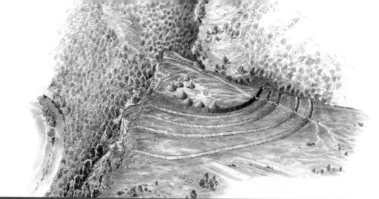

Hillforts above the Wye

The hillfort at Symonds Yat is one of at least nine prehistoric hilltop enclosures dotted along the lower Wye Valley. These earthworks, constructed between 700BC – 43AD are a tangible link to our prehistoric past and a striking reminder of the people who once gathered here. Although most Iron Age people lived in small farmsteads, they also constructed enclosures surrounded by banks and ditches. These sites overlooked the river and were visible from the surrounding countryside. At Symonds Yat the hillfort was defended on two sides by steep cliffs and on the third by five concentric ramparts, each a substantial bank with a ditch alongside.

We don't know what their exact use was, but the size of these hillforts suggests they were as much a statement about the prestige of the inhabitants as a defensive place. So although we call them hillforts it is likely they were much more than places to retreat to in times of tribal trouble. They were probably the local focus for politics, religion and trade.

Wye Tourists, eager to interpret legends handed down over generations, had their own theories. The Rev. T. D. Fosbrooke wrote that the nearby Little Doward hillfort, 'is a valuable reminder of British fortification, where Caractacus probably posted himself, for how otherwise are the adjacent Roman camps on the Great Doward and Symonds Yat to be accounted for?'.

As Fosbroke recognised, some of these hillforts face each other in pairs, either side of the Wye (although Fosbrooke was wrong about the Roman connection). We don't know if the Wye actually marked the border between the Dobunni and the Silures tribes; or whether they were designed to control the river Wye itself – and its valuable trade. But there are pairs, Symonds Yat facing the Little Doward, and Piercefield facing Spital Meend, as well as the promontory fort at Bulwark, which controlled the mouth of the Wye.

'The Ross and Monmouth Line...though only twelve and a half miles long, affords the prettiest dozen miles of railway scenery in England.' Symonds Yat station c. 1910. (Monmouth Museum)

Symonds Yat East
Trows and trains

From Yat Rock tourists walked down the mule track to New Weir, where they would find their boats waiting for them just above the weir. The weir diverted water to power New Weir ironworks on the other side of the river. Following the Navigation Acts the owner of the ironworks had to provide a lock so that boats could pass the weir.

The novelty of the trows passing through the lock intrigued the tourists and afforded 'some amusement to the minds of those who are not in the habit of witnessing such scenes', wrote Charles Heath. 'On opening the gates, after the vessel is lowered to the level of the river, the current sets into the lock, in opposition to the stream. In order therefore to bring her into the tide the same force is necessary. No sooner is the signal made for assistance than young and old, boys and girls fly to the rope, and, with a zeal most hearty, soon deliver the vessel from her otherwise stationary situation, to the active current of the river. The boatmen reward their exertions by giving a few of them a half penny a piece'. Nothing remains of the lock today, and even the weir has been artificially altered to enhance the rapids for canoeists.

More evidence survives of the railway which ran through Symonds Yat from 1873 to 1959. Going south passengers enjoyed the picturesque views along the river bank towards Monmouth. Today the Wye Valley Walk and Peregrine Path cycleway follow this route. The station occupied the space in front of the Royal Hotel, which is now a car park. To go north the navvies tunnelled under Symonds Yat Rock so that trains left the station and entered a tunnel behind the Forest View Hotel, emerging under Coldwell Rocks.

The arrival of the railway meant Symonds Yat became one of the most popular destinations along the Wye. Here the tourist's every need was catered for – from boat trips to fishing and even butterfly collecting! The Doward was a favoured destination amongst Victorian butterfly collectors who chartered special excursion trains to Symonds Yat. Local boys collected rare Purple Emperors and other butterflies and sold them to enthusiastic collectors at the station.

Edwardian elegance at Symonds Yat c. 1904. The little cream shed was a waiting room hanging out over the riverbank. (Neil Parkhouse Collection)

'an immense Iron-forge and slitting Mill, disgorging its black sulphureous smoke'

James Wathen's sketch shows a row of worker's cottages above the ironworks, shortly before it closed around 1800, 'to the great loss of many industrious families'. When Thomas Roscoe passed in 1839 all was 'tranquil…the works are pulled down, and the population gone'. (Herefordshire Archive Service)

The New Weir diverted water from the river to fill the forge pond. This fed waterwheels which powered the bellows and hammers at the ironworks. A trow is moored above the forge pond in this watercolour by Michael Angelo Rooker c. 1789. (Monmouth Museum)

New Weir Forge
Mr Partridge's Ironworks

This 'immense Iron-forge and slitting Mill, disgorging its black sulphureous smoke' captured the tourists' attention at New Weir. The forge was probably established in the 1570s by the Earl of Shrewsbury. John Partridge, 'Ironmonger of Ross' took over the lease in 1753. He came from a family of ironmasters, owning furnaces at Bishopswood and Lydbrook too. The forge processed and refined cast iron from nearby furnaces. A slitting mill cut iron into rods to be made into nails. This was one of many interconnected metal making sites in the Wye Valley and Forest of Dean.

Fascinated by the industry along the river tourists left wonderful descriptions of what they saw. Whately who took the tour in 1770 described how, 'In the midst of all this gloom is an iron forge, covered with a black cloud of smoak, and surrounded with half burned ore, with coal, and with cinders; the fuel for it is brought down a path, worn into steps narrow and steep, and winding among precipices; and near it is an open space of barren moor, about which are scattered the huts of the workmen.'

The number of illustrations of New Weir show just how popular this location was with the visitors. They appreciated the picturesque composition of rocky outcrops, wooded slopes and industry. Nature has reclaimed much of New Weir Forge, but if you wander around the site try and imagine 'the sullen sound from the strokes of the great hammers of the forge' echoing through the smoky woods.

Detail from Samuel Ireland's New Weir, 1797, showing horses pulling a trow towards the lock on the left bank. The ironworks are on the right bank. (Chepstow Museum)

Thoracles and truckles, corbolas and cobles

Thoracles, truckles, corbolas and cobles – these are just some of the local names given to an unusual type of fishing craft which was once a common sight on the Wye – the coracle. They were viewed with much intrigue by the Wye Tourists. The Duke of Rutland spotted them at New Weir in 1805: 'peculiar to this part of the river… we saw two men going out in their coricles to fish. Each man lays hold of one end of a net, about 20 yards long, and paddles down the river, till they feel a strike. They then haul it up as quick as possible, and draw it on shore. They paddle at a great rate, and put us in mind of what we read concerning the Indians in their canoes.'

The earliest coracles were made of woven willow twigs covered in horse-hide, although later ones were ribbed with laths and covered with pitch canvas. A paddle was held in one hand, leaving the other hand free to fish. Sometimes pairs of coracles worked the river together. Being extremely light the fishermen would put the coracles on their shoulders to carry them home. At one time a fish house stood on the river bank a little way below New Weir forge, where Gilpin

remarked, 'the men employed in the salmon fishery use the little round boats, called Truckles which the least motion will upset and the slightest touch may destroy'.

Tourists were told of one adventurous coracle man from Wilton, near Ross. In the 1730s a trowman called Luke Hughes kept an inn at Wilton, where he catered for the travelling tradesmen and watermen using the river. To settle a bet Luke paddled a coracle down the Wye, into the Bristol Channel, around the island of Lundy and back – in two weeks! Tom O'Neill was another coracle maker and fisherman who had a reputation as a 'most inveterate Salmon poacher'. He was said to have lived in a cave between Monmouth and Symonds Yat.

William Dew from Kerne Bridge was still coracle fishing with a rod and line until about 1910. These craft disappeared from the river after World War 1.

Top: Coracles at Ross in the late 19th century. (Monmouth Museum)

Timber!

The woodlands of the Wye have been carefully managed for hundreds, if not thousands, of years. They were coppiced on an industrial scale to supply the local metal making industries with the vast quantities of charcoal they needed. Charles Heath described how 'every ten or twelve years, the woods, are cropped quite close to the ground, principally to supply the forges and furnaces with charcoal'. This intensive use of the woods created many tensions, not least that the views the tourists admired were 'deprived of their former interest'.

The timber trade was especially valuable in the early 18th century when the Navy appointed agents to source much of its ship building timber from the Wye Valley and the Forest of Dean. When Nelson toured the Wye in 1802 he bemoaned the felling of young trees and ordered the replanting of the Forest of Dean, suggesting 'the first thing necessary…is to plant some acres of acorns'. These acorns have grown into the mature trees at the heart of the Forest of Dean.

Lumberjacks and woodmen moved the timber to the river on wagons and sledges. The largest logs were rafted together and floated down to the timber yards and sawpits at Chepstow. In 1827 it was reported that the Chepstow

firm of Bowsher, Hodges and Watkins supplied half of all the timber used by the Navy. Between 1830 and 1856 Chepstow was a bonded port for timber and a high stone wall enclosed the timber yard, which occupied most of the river bank below the bridge.

Now that the woods are not so intensively managed the landscape of the Wye Valley looks more natural than it has done for centuries. It has become one of the most important areas in Europe for woodland conservation, brimming with native trees and rare species such as large-leaved lime.

Cliffs at Coldwell Rocks.

Lime kiln below the limestone cliffs at New Weir, c. 1815. (Chepstow Museum)

'It is worthy of remark, how suddenly the banks of the WYE acquire their fine picturesque outline, when the river enters the Mountain Lime. The abrupt eminences which are the constant features of that formation, here twist and drive the bed of the river into the most tortuous windings, and coop it up like a prisoner between their craggy walls.

Louisa Ann Twamley, 1838

Limestone cliffs towering above the river are a distinctive feature of the lower Wye Valley landscape. This limestone was formed from the shell fragments of millions of dead sea creatures deposited on the floor of a warm shallow sea some 350 million years ago. Over a long period of time, as successive layers formed those underneath became buried and compacted. The cliffs were created much later when the river cut down through the layers. Little Doward is one of a few places in the area where the complete geological succession from the late Early Devonian to the Early Carboniferous, a time span of roughly 55 million years, is accessible.

Limestone has been a valuable resource in the Wye Valley, as the scars on the landscape, especially around Symonds Yat, illustrate. In 1818 the local tour guide and writer Thomas Dudley Fosbroke moaned that the Doward was 'gormandized by the ravenous lime-kiln... regardless of the beauty of the Wye'. Charles Heath grumbled that, 'The beauty and quiet of this scene has lately received considerable diminution, by the erection of an extensive Lime-Kiln just below (Coldwell Rocks), – the effluvia from which is not only disagreeable in itself, but obscures by its smoke the appearance, in some places of those beautiful greens, with which the rocks are clothed, and for which they are so peculiarly admired'.

'Galleried throughout by quarries, and rendered wildly beautiful by the misty smoke from its numerous kilns', wrote Thomas Roscoe in 1839 of the Doward. The scars of quarrying and several banks of limekilns are still visible in this photo c. 1885. (Neil Parkhouse Collection)

Some of the quarried limestone was used for building. Some was crushed and used to improve road surfaces. The rest was burnt in limekilns which processed the lime so it could be used to spread on fields to improve the soil or as lime mortar used for building.

The Halls who toured the Wye around 1860 remarked on 'the workman's tool ringing through the air as he forces the limestone from the mass, to burn in lime-kilns, picturesquely scattered on the hillside.' But lime burning was far from picturesque. It was a dangerous job and workers were often burnt by the lime which could explode unexpectedly.

Today these inaccessible cliffs provide feeding, nesting and breeding areas for many spectacular birds of prey including goshawks, peregrine falcons and buzzards. Rare whitebeams and sessile oak stands grow on the limestone, whilst an area of limestone pavement on the Little Doward provides important habitats for lime-loving plants and animals.

Mules carrying charcoal up to the limekilns at New Weir, c. 1860

Excavating the Hyena's Den c. 1871.
(Monmouth Museum)

Slippery Jim and his wife Betsy.
(Courtesy of Gerald Gardiner)

Great Doward
Slippery Jim and the Hyena's Den

When hyena remains were found in a limestone cave on the Doward they attracted the attention of a well-known Victorian geologist – the Reverend William Samuel Symonds. Miners looking for iron ore had discovered the bones in King Arthur's Cave, which soon became known as the Hyena's Den. A local man who went by the name of Slippery Jim or Jem the Slipper, helped Reverend Symonds locate the Hyena's Den in 1871. Jim lived with his wife in another nearby cavern.

Symond's excavations removed large amounts of material from the cave, debris that had accumulated over thousands of years. Unlike modern archaeologists, Symonds excavated in a very destructive way. He used dynamite to blast layers of concrete-like stalagmite deposits from the cave floor, discovering bones from lion, horse, giant deer and hyena. Well below the 19th century floor level he found the bones of Ice Age animals – woolly rhinoceros, cave bear and mammoth. 'It was clear from

Removing debris c. 1871. (Monmouth Museum)

Above: Slippery Jim. (Dean Heritage Museum Trust)
Left: William Symonds, born in Hereford 1818, was a founder member of the Woolhope Naturalist's Club. They organised excursions to sites of interest in the Wye Valley and their notes provide a delightful insight into the age of the Victorian enthusiast. This lives on, as the Club continues to this day.

the state of the bones that the cave had been the resort of hyenas, as many of them had evidently been dragged in and gnawed,' wrote Rev. Symonds. He also reported how a local farmer had 'for some time manured his fields with bones of extinct animals which ages ago ranged over his holding'!

The variety of animal remains found here helps to illustrate how the climate has changed. In the colder periods mammoths and woolly rhinoceros were common; during warmer times hyena and deer thrived. In the last Ice Age when this area was on the edge of the tundra the Hyena's Den provided shelter for humans too. Bones found during the excavations suggest that some 12,000 years ago they sat around a fire eating red deer. So Slippery Jim, who boasted he had lived in his cave for 30 years (and not washed during that period), was following a long tradition of cave dwellers.

Jim and his wife Betsy were probably the last cave dwellers on the Doward. Betsy picked wild strawberries and sold them to tourists at Symonds Yat. Jim made fur slippers from the skin of animals he trapped (hence the name Slipper) to sell as souvenirs. It was probably in these caves that the 'inveterate Salmon poacher' Tom O' Neill lived too. The caves were formed by a river flowing along the base of the limestone cliffs. Over time water dissolved the limestone creating caverns like King Arthur's Cave and Merlin's Cave.

Right: Woolly rhinoceros teeth, found during Rev. Symonds' excavation. (Hereford Museum & Art Gallery)

38

Deer now roam across Blakemore's picturesque park at Wyastone Leys.

Wyastone Leys, on the banks of the Wye, was rebuilt in the 1860s.

Little Doward
Victorian Vandal

When Richard Blakemore, a wealthy Victorian ironmaster, moved to the Little Doward in 1820 he came with grand ideas. Undoubtedly influenced by notions of the picturesque he set about designing a new landscape around his home at Wyastone Leys. Removing commoners' rights and enclosing common land on the Doward to create his parkland, Blakemore thought nothing of blasting through cliffs to form a picturesque chasm. The holes in the rock face where the dynamite was placed are still visible today. Blakemore was a bit of a Victorian vandal as his landscaped walks and carriage drives cut straight through the ramparts of an ancient hillfort. As the local vicar reported, Blakemore was 'entirely unacquainted with the antiquarian interest attached to his property'.

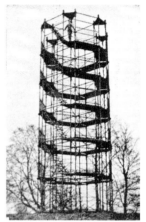

Above: Looking through the ramparts of the upper enclosure. Top right: To enjoy the view towards Monmouth visitors were allowed to climb the steps of Blakemore's Folly on Sunday evenings. (Monmouth Museum)

The 'peculiarly fine outline' of Little Doward hillfort from the Monmouth road, which Thomas Fosbroke described in 1818, is obscured by woodland today. But the Iron Age hillfort remains a striking feature on the summit, 724 feet above the Wye. There are two parts to the enclosure, now divided by a sunken trackway which runs across the site. A single massive rampart surrounds the upper enclosure. The lower enclosure does not have a rampart, but has steep cliffs on three sides.

The banks and ditches surrounding the fort were probably as much a statement of the prestige of the people who lived here during the Iron Age as Blakemore's picturesque landscaping was in the 19th century. The crowning glory of his estate was 'a curious observatory, erected upon a rock, and constructed of iron trestlework of an open pattern, with a winding staircase inside'. This 70 foot tower would have provided an excellent platform from which to view the hillfort and surrounding landscape. But compared to the Iron Age monument which has survived for 2000 years, Blakemore's Folly lasted for less than a hundred years. It was dismantled in the early 1900s and reused in the construction of Whitchurch village hall. You can still follow Blakemore's picturesque paths which were 'formed with taste' and have the 'most extensive and varied views of the surrounding counties'. The rusting iron gates along the way provide a reminder of this ironmaster's attempts to 'improve' the landscape.

A toggle found during excavations in 2009. Made from deer antler, it may be 2000 years old and was probably used just like a duffle coat toggle to fasten clothing or bags.

The Little Doward hillfort may have looked like this. There is evidence of metalworking and finds include Iron Age pottery and animal bones. Because of the limestone bedrock the bone finds are very well preserved, including some worked bone dice. Burnt grain found here shows that crops were also cultivated and processed.

Arriving in Monmouth by coach, perhaps after an excursion to Raglan Castle, c. 1840. (Monmouth Museum)

Monmouth
Halfway

As the halfway stage on the Wye Tour many tourists stayed at one of the inns in Agincourt Square, although a few slept on their boats. The Beaufort Arms, the town's main coaching inn, was the favoured place to stay, especially after Nelson slept there in 1802. Mr Tibbs who owned the Beaufort in the late eighteenth century, created a pleasure ground on the Vauxhall fields. 'Here when the weather permits', John Byng noted in 1781, 'the company of all the neighbourhood meet, every Thursday, at 5 o'clock in the evening; and dance till 9 o'clock upon two bowling greens, from which the views are delightfull'. According to Francis Grose in 1775, 'The price of this Entertainment is two shillings to Strangers for which they have tea Coffee & Musick'.

Plenty of tourists found the castle where King Henry V was born a disappointment. William Gilpin was especially saddened that 'the birth-place of a mighty prince... is now

Agincourt Square as the tourists would have found it in 1808. Many visited Charles Heath's shop here or stayed in the hotels which overlooked the square, such as the King's Head.

The bark house and wharves at Monmouth
c. 1880s. (Monmouth Museum)

The *Monmouth*, a 210 ton brig, was built in
1825 for merchants in Bristol. When she was
launched she 'lurched and several persons
were thrown into the water, two boys being
drowned'. She voyaged to Nevis, Trieste and
the West Indies during the 1830s and 40s,
but was lost off the south coast of Cuba in
1852. (Monmouth Museum)

converted into a yard for fatting ducks'. Tourists, including
Nelson and Lady Hamilton, went to Charles Heath's shop
in Agincourt Square where they could purchase a selection
of his guidebooks. As well as exploring Monmouth and The
Kymin, the town was also a base for excursions to the
nearby ruins of Raglan Castle and Llanthony Abbey. As
Leitch Ritchie noted in 1839 the tourist '...while at
Monmouth...has an opportunity ...of making himself
acquainted with many interesting objects which ought to
be considered as adjuncts of the tour of the Wye'.

Alighting from their boats visitors would have seen the
wharves either side of the Wye Bridge, the bark store, the
timber yard and the boat building businesses. This inland
town had a long tradition of boatbuilding and Thomas
Swift, who came from a family of ship builders and boat
men, was said to have been the greatest shipbuilder on
the Wye. The Swift family ran regular trows to Bristol.
Some truly massive boats were built at Monmouth
including the 386 ton *Bolivar* in 1826. She would have
needed flood water and high tides to reach the Severn.

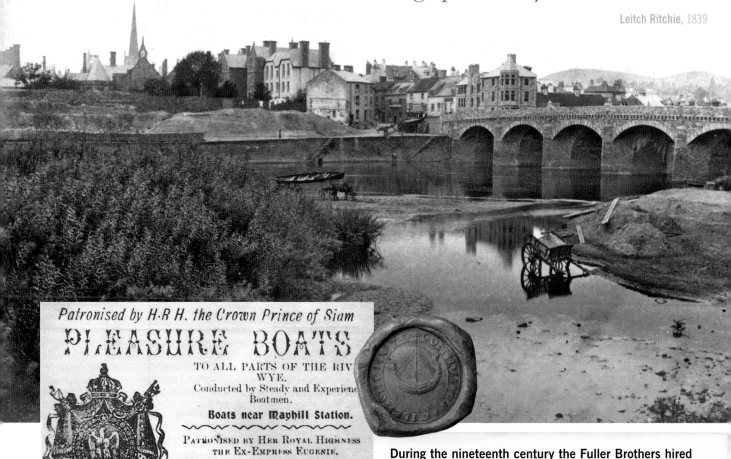

'Monmouth, as the half-way station between Ross and Chepstow for the tourists of the Wye, usually claims a large portion of their attention.'

Leitch Ritchie, 1839

Top: Looking towards the Waterman's Arms and Wye Bridge c. 1880. (Neil Parkhouse Collection)
Above: Advertisement from the Monmouthshire Beacon. Inset: Monmouth's medieval seal shows a masted boat similar to a trow, illustrating how important the river trade was to this inland port. (Both images Monmouth Museum)

During the nineteenth century the Fuller Brothers hired boats out from the Wye Bridge. The Fullers ran the Waterman's Arms, traditional haunt of the bow hauliers and watermen, which stood on the riverfront beside the bridge. This photo from around 1880 shows a horse trailer loaded with a rowing boat at Monmouth. Although Fuller's boatmen could punt boats upriver all the way from Chepstow, hired boats were sometimes returned by road. A man called Jacky Raggy provided a regular service using a two wheeled frame drawn by a pony. Above the bridge cottages lined the wharf, where there was a small inlet to allow the boatmen to moor up close to their homes. They were demolished when the A40 was constructed.

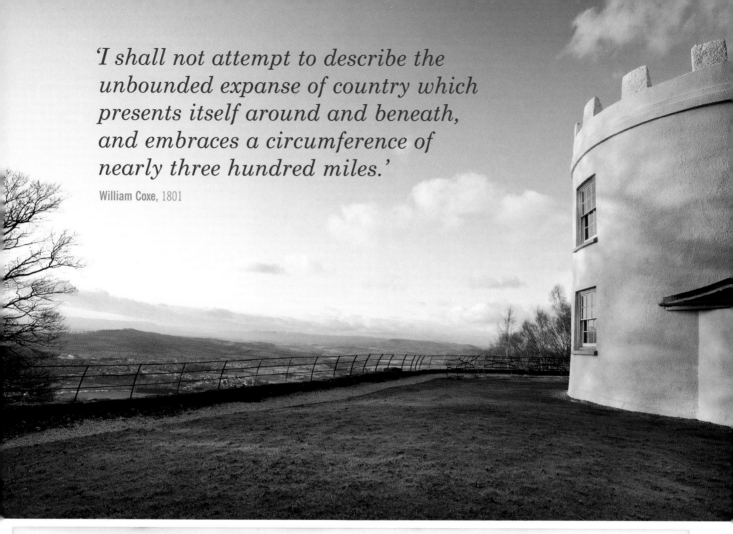

> *'I shall not attempt to describe the unbounded expanse of country which presents itself around and beneath, and embraces a circumference of nearly three hundred miles.'*
>
> William Coxe, 1801

The Kymin

A picturesque picnic place

Perhaps the most famous Wye Tourist was Nelson, who took the excursion from Ross to Monmouth in 1802.
He visited the Kymin, the much famed viewpoint overlooking Monmouth where a Naval Temple, honouring notable 18th century admirals, had been recently erected. As his tour boat, decorated with laurel leaves, came into view on the river below, cannons boomed out from the Temple to greet him.

A two-storey circular Georgian banqueting house adorned the summit of the Kymin where Nelson enjoyed a 'handsome' breakfast. As the picturesque movement flourished it became fashionable to build summerhouses at sites with spectacular viewpoints. The Round House was constructed in 1794 by the Monmouth Picnic Club. Guests received instructions on how to observe the views correctly and Charles Heath produced a guidebook which described the views from each window as they lined up with notable beauty spots. A series of walks with seats had been laid out in the surrounding woodland 'presenting the country in the most picturesque manner'.

Top: The Round House on the Kymin.

Tinplate furnace men with the tools of
their trade – long tongues.

Women and boys worked here too. The younger
men and boys were generally employed in the
tin house or wash house. Women separated the
rolled sheets of iron, using a special long, knife-
like implement called a 'separator's knife'.
(Both images Monmouth Museum)

Redbrook
Copper pennies and tin plates

**It might be hard to imagine now, but since Roman times
Redbrook has been a hive of industrial activity.** First iron,
then copper, and later tinplate were made here. This
tributary of the Wye once ran red with iron ore.

Around 1680 a local man, John Coster, experimented with
new ways of smelting copper using coal rather than
charcoal. At this time Britain was dependent on expensive
copper imports, so when Coster perfected the process and
established a coal-fired smelter in Redbrook in 1690 he
revolutionised Britain's copper smelting industry. By 1697
it was reported that there were ships at Chepstow 'laden
with Copper-ore from Cornwall, bound for Redbrook'. Coster
was now producing 80 tons of the highest quality copper,
which sold for £100 a ton and was even exported to Holland.

In 1692 the English Copper Company established works
in Redbrook too. Securing contracts from the Mint, they

Above left: In the 20th century the village ran to the tune of the Works' hooter: 6.50am wake up blast, 7am starting hooter, 8.30am breakfast, 12.30pm lunch, and 4.30pm home. (Monmouth Museum)
Above: The Tinplate Works around 1860 when Mr and Mrs Hall toured the Wye.

stamped out the blanks for copper coins, becoming the government's main supplier. These were the most important copper works in the country and Redbrook soon became Britain's copper capital. The impact on the people who lived here was profound. The copper ores were roasted to drive off sulphur and arsenic, and visitors commented that, 'a thick yellow smoke hangs over the works which is very unwholesome as well as detrimental to vegetation'. Despite this tourists passing in 1798 thought that Redbrook was 'the most bustling little place imaginable' where everyone was 'grilled in daily smoke and flame' and 'quiet was here wholly banished by the reverberating strokes from the iron-works'.

In the 19th and 20th centuries Redbrook became famous for its tin – the thinnest tin you could buy. The first tinplate was made here in 1774. David Tanner, a local ironmaster, bought the vacant copper works and converted to tinplate manufacture in the 1790s. By 1848 Samuel Lewis wrote that, 'Redbrook ...is now celebrated for the manufacture of tin plates, of which from 400 to 500 boxes are produced weekly; there is also an iron-foundry. In these works about 120 men are constantly employed.'

Tinplate from Redbrook was used to make tin cans and tin boxes. With the establishment of the Redbrook Tinplate Company the brand became famous around the world. Much of the demand came from the United States where it was used for packing tobacco. By 1949 43,500 boxes of tinplate were produced weekly and exported worldwide. The noise from the rolling mills, which operated around the clock, could be heard for miles around. Redbrook's residents lived cheek by jowl with the sound, smell and smoke from the Works until 1961 when, unable to compete with the new Welsh strip mills, the Tinplate Works closed.

A horse drawn tramroad from Monmouth to Coleford was constructed in 1810, bringing coal from the Forest of Dean mines down to the Wye at Redbrook. A branch line ran down to the wharf and works, crossing this bridge along a steep self-acting incline. (Chepstow Museum)

What a waste!

Centuries of metal making in Redbrook produced huge amounts of waste. Thomas Burgham, ironmaster at Redbrook from 1828 to 1870, calculated the waste cinders here amounted to over 500 years' of smelting. Most waste products were recycled. Copper slag was purchased by the Turnpike Trusts to improve the roads. Slag was crushed and bought by Bristol glass makers, who owned the *Susanna* (built at Chepstow in 1784) to transport the waste to Bristol. The molten waste from copper-smelting was cast into copings, quoin stones and slag blocks. You can spot these dark blocks in buildings along the Wye.

Above: Puddingstones that missed the boat (or trow)! (adventa)

Right: Some family names, like Hudson, have a long association with the local millstone industry. Noah Hudson was probably the last millstone maker in Penallt, a job he combined with work at the tinplate works in Redbrook in the early 20th century. (Phil Hudson)

Penallt
True Grit – the millstone industry of the Wye Valley

South of Monmouth, between Penallt and Llandogo, a very hard quartz conglomerate rock, known locally as puddingstone, outcrops. Like a natural concrete this rock is very abrasive, making it ideal for millstones.

Penallt was once famous for its millstones. Traditionally millstones ground corn, but this was an important cider producing area. Charles Heath mentions the 'rich orcharding and fruit trees, producing the best kinds of cider and perry' along the Wye. The rough puddingstone was especially good for cider millstones and most farms had a puddingstone press to make their own cider. Cider played a significant role in everyday life: farm workers were often paid in cider and it was even used to baptise babies.

Leitch Ritchie, who took the Wye Tour in 1839, described the local cider mills as 'consisting of a circular stone, about twelve hundred weight, set on its edge in a shallow circular trough, and drawn

Left: Prisk Wood on the left, with Redbrook centre and the Kymin beyond.
Above: Cider press at the Anchor, Tintern. (Monmouth Museum)

round by a horse. The apples are gradually introduced into the trough, and a quantity may be thus mashed... The expressed juice is put into casks, not quite filled, and in the open air; and as soon as the vinous fermentation takes place, it is racked. When two years old it may be bottled, after which it will become rich and sparkling, and so remain for twenty or thirty years.'

These hillsides echoed to the tap, tap, tap of the millstone maker's chisels hitting stone. Records from 1647 show that a toll of fourpence had to be paid to the Lord of Striguil in Chepstow for every pair of millstones transported down river from Redbrook. One of the earliest references to a millstone hewer in Penallt is George Younge in 1684.

Where the quartz conglomerate outcrops in Prisk Wood at Penallt (reached via the old railway bridge at Redbrook) a maze of abandoned millstone quarry workings litter the hillside. At the mouth of each of the deep gullies cut into the slope you can find flattened level areas which were used as working platforms to craft the millstones. The finished stones were rolled down the hill to the loading point on the riverbank. A large piece of wood was probably put through the central hole in the stones to help control their movement. Some missed the boat, quite literally, and now lie in the river!

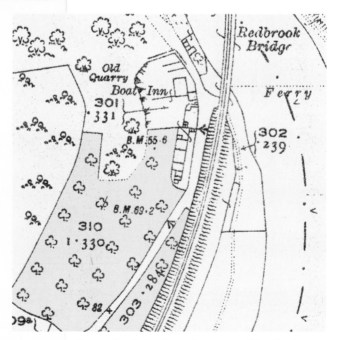

Orchards, lining Lone Lane near The Boat, are shown in green on this 19th century map.

One of the papermills around 1902.
(Neil Parkhouse Collection)

Old paper warehouses where the Whitebrook
flows into the Wye c. 1925. Eighteen bags of
rags, sent down from Monmouth and recorded
in the account book of the Hereford trow, the
Charles in 1825, would have been unloaded
here to be used in the paper mills. (Neil
Parkhouse Collection)

Whitebrook
'A busy station of paper mills'

**The next tributary cascading to join the Wye is the
Whitebrook.** It powered wireworks and paper mills. The
wireworks were set up in 1607 at a cost of £900, by the
Company of Mineral and Battery Works, who also ran the
wireworks in Tintern. Wire was a valuable commodity and
much sought after to make carding combs, nails, horse
harnesses and the farthingales and stomachers of
Elizabethan fashion.

When Thomas Roscoe passed the village in 1837 he
mentioned 'a busy station of paper mills'. Paper
manufacture, which used rags rather than woodpulp, had
replaced wire making around 1760 and by 1793 there
were as many as six paper mills lining the Whitebrook.
They made high grade paper for bank notes. The last mill
closed around 1880, but the ruins of the paper mills, the
grand houses of the mill owners, and the ponds which
stored the water needed to power the waterwheels still line
the banks of the Whitebrook.

'Independent of the gratification it will afford the lover of fine scenery, the road promises to be of incalculable advantage to the counties of Monmouth and Gloucester.'

Gloucester Journal, 1825

Bigsweir
Turnpikes and tolls

In 1824 a Turnpike Trust was established to build a road between St Arvans and Redbrook. To carry the road over the Wye a 160 foot cast iron arch formed an elegant bridge at Bigsweir. Trows carried the metal segments of the bridge upriver because, until this point, there was no road along the valley. The river had been the main transport route connecting villages on the Wye for more than two thousand years.

When the 'Gentlemen of the Trust' (who included local ironmaster David Mushet) dined at the Beaufort Arms in Monmouth on August 16th 1828 they were probably celebrating the opening of the turnpike and the benefits 'by which lime and coal from Dean Forest will be introduced at considerably less than the present cost into a large district of Monmouthshire.'

To cross the bridge at Bigsweir on foot cost a penny or sixpence for a coach or carriage. The Royal Family, Royal Mail carriers, soldiers and people going to church on

Top: Turnpike road crossing Bigsweir Bridge c. 1840. (Chepstow Museum) Above: The bridge was designed in London by Charles Hollis and cast in Merthyr Tydfil.

Sunday were exempt! The tolls were used to maintain the roads and to provide a profit for the shareholders of the Turnpike Trust. Tolls were abolished in 1879 putting William Parry, the last Bigsweir toll keeper, out of a job. One of his sons, James, was still living with his widowed mother in the tollhouse in 1917. Now it is inhabited only by bats, albeit rare and protected ones!

'There twice a day the Severn fills,
The salt seawater passes by
And hushes half the babbling Wye,
And makes a silence in the hills.'

Tennyson, 1833

Trows transporting timber at Llandogo.
W. H. Bartlett, 1835.

All aboard for the Whitebrook and District Choir
outing, Llandogo c. 1913. (Roger Brown)

Llandogo
Waiting for the tide

Nearly all the tourists disliked the muddy river below Bigsweir where 'the Wye becomes a tide stream, acted upon by the ebb and flow of the Severn sea,' as Leitch Ritchie described it in 1839. Llandogo was the highest that large 50 ton trows could reach with a little help from the tide. Clark's 1866 Guide to Monmouth reported that, 'Good sized sloops make their way from the Bristol Channel to this place.' A shingle beach exposed at low tide on the Gloucestershire side of the river was the favoured place for trows to wait for the tide.

The regular trip for Llandogo's watermen was down the Wye, across the Severn and up the Avon to Bristol. Here cargoes were unloaded at the 'Welsh Back' wharf (where you could always find a boat back to Wales), beside a pub called the Llandoger Trow. Bristol, with its international connections, was the main market for goods from the riverside villages of the Wye.

Trows were the life blood of the village and between the 1780s and the 1860s twenty-eight ships, trows and barges were owned by Llandogo families. Mariner George Williams owned four trows when he died in 1883 (the *Good Hope*, the *Hannah Louisa*, the *Eagle* and the *George and Mary*). Alfred Fryer Washbourn Williams was the last Sea Captain of trows out of Llandogo. He was born in The Sloop in 1877 and when he died in 1953 he was buried in the village churchyard alongside generations of river men. The bell of the last Llandogo trow, the *William & Sarah* built in 1860, now hangs in St. Oudoceus Church.

The river was the focus of village life. Boats were built and sails repaired on the riverside; women cleaned oak bark; nimble–footed donkeys carried goods from the quayside up a maze of steps to cottages high above the river; and the watermen and bow hauliers whiled away time waiting for the tide in their favourite watering holes – The Sloop and The Ship. It was a way of life killed off when the railway arrived.

High above Llandogo the waterfall at Cleddon was a popular beauty spot, reached by a circuitous path from the village. Close by, the Bread and Cheese Stones, supposedly named for their resemblance to a loaf of bread and chunk of cheese, are thought to have been the spot where William Wordsworth was inspired to write *'Lines composed a few miles above Tintern Abbey'*. He may even have sat on these stones! This was traditionally a lookout for local residents, who could see the trows coming up the river from Brockweir and race down to the quay to get work unloading cargo.

Trows were also used for pleasure trips and there are reports of workers from the Whitebrook paper mills going by Llandogo Trow on an outing to Bristol Zoo. Trows were still being used in the early twentieth century for pleasure trips from Llandogo:

'On Friday, August 17th, in connection with the Whitebrook Baptist Sunday School, the barge *Mary Jane* (kindly lent for the occasion by Mr William Pick) sailed for Beachley. Leaving the shore at Mr George Hodges yard, Llandogo at 8 am with about 150 on board, the order came to let go the ropes and the excursionists were soon gliding over the waters of the beautiful River Wye. The Whitelye Brass Band, who gave kindly their services for the day, commenced playing 'We are out on the ocean sailing'. (Monmouthshire Beacon, 25th August 1895)

The *George and Mary*

Although she was built in Newport in 1851, the *George and Mary* had a long connection with Llandogo. She was sold to the Williams family around 1869 and became a familiar feature on the Llandogo riverside. In the face of competition from the railways some trows were adapted to become seagoing vessels and the bulwarks on the *George and Mary* were built up. The newer timbers are clearly visible in this photograph from around 1905.

Top: The *George and Mary* waiting for the tide on the Gloucester bank, Llandogo.
Left: This drowned trow c. 1910 is probably the *George and Mary*. She slowly rotted away on the Gloucester bank. (Both images Neil Parkhouse Collection)

Salmon and stop nets

All in an April evening...

In the 1860s two Scottish salmon fishermen leased the fishing rights between Monmouth and Chepstow from the Duke of Beaufort. The Miller brothers moved to Llandogo and established a very successful business, sending their catch of Wye salmon, in woven rush baskets, to top London hotels and Billingsgate Fish Market.

Alexander Miller was an early pioneer for conservation, campaigning against the destruction of young fish and poaching in the Wye, a problem which continued well into the 20th century.

A traditional method of salmon fishing on the tidal sections of the Wye involved the use of stop nets – 'two long poles some 18 feet long fixed together like a pair of compasses with a net shaped like a purse fastened between them'. The stop net season ran from April to August.

A 2500 mile journey ends every April in Llandogo. Elvers (baby eels) start life in the Gulf of Mexico. They swim across the Atlantic and three years later find their way into the river Wye, coming upstream with the incoming spring tides. They remain in the river for about seven years, before a return trip is made to the Gulf to spawn and die.

It is said the best elvers in the world are caught in Llandogo and for hundreds of years local fishermen waited on the riverbank with large nets, ready to scoop the slithering mass from the water as the elvers reached the village. Once caught they were made into a 'cheese', by pressing all the slime and water out, washing them and cooking before another pressing through a fine muslin to form the 'cheese'. Slices of cheese were then fried in bacon fat. Over the last 50 years elvering has changed from being an annual village tradition, to a commercial operation undertaken by outsiders who export the elvers to Japan where they are an expensive delicacy.

Above: Poachers on the upper reaches of the Wye, 1930s.

Top: Stop net fishing at Brockweir in the 1950s.
(Chepstow Museum)

Edward Dayes painted large stacks of bark on the river bank at Chepstow c. 1800. At this time 5000 tons of bark were being exported annually. (Chepstow Museum)

Above: Bark rick on the river bank adjacent to a trow at Llandogo c. 1880. (Neil Parkhouse Collection) Right: Women liked to sing whilst they cleaned the bark. (Bewdley Museum) Right: Barking Irons. (Monmouth Museum)

Barking up the wrong tree

When Robert Bloomfield came down the Wye in 1807 he saw 'dark brown saplings flayed alive'. This was the aftermath of the bark harvest, which took place between April and June. Bark was a valuable source of tannin used to process raw animal hides into leather.

Metal spoons with wooden handles, called barking irons, levered the bark off the trees. They were left to die over the summer before felling for their timber. Men wearing 'a cross between a life bouy and a horse-collar' carried the bark to the riverside where the women stripped the moss, lichen and outer skin off. Thomas Roscoe commented on the 'groups of women and children, busily engaged in barking the fallen timber who sent forth many a peal of merry-cadenced laughter'. The bark was stacked beside the river in huge piles, like a hayrick, ready to be loaded onto trows and taken to local tanneries

Around 1714 bark began to be exported through Chepstow to tanneries in Ireland. Exports grew rapidly and returning ships brought back iron ore from Lancashire for the Valley's ironworks. At least 5000 tons of bark went through Chepstow annually by 1800, when there were a number of bark merchants in the town. By this time it was such an important industry that the port of Chepstow regulated the price of oak bark across the UK.

Brockweir

'A city of refuge for persons of desperate and lawless character'

Life on the river might seem romantic today, but until the middle of the 19th century the 'men of the river' had a very bad reputation. This was mostly due to the bow hauliers who worked in gangs; sometimes as many as ten were needed to pull the biggest and most heavily laden trows. They frequented the Wyeside taverns which served the passing river traffic. When water levels were low they could be stuck for days on end, and with little room for stocks of food on board the inns had a captive audience.

Brockweir was the main transhipment point on the Wye, located beside a weir past which the largest trows could not navigate. With at least sixteen pubs, the village had a terrible reputation for the drunkenness of the river men. It was 'a refuge for persons of desperate and lawless character'. In an attempt to save their souls a church was established in the village by the Moravians in 1832. Perhaps to emphasize a point they built it on the site of the cock-fighting pit!

Almost all the villagers were employed on the river or in riverside trades. Many trows, brigs, sloops and schooners were made here up to the end of the 19th century, including the *Constantine*, a barque of 506 tons, built by the Monmouth ship builder Thomas Swift and launched in 1847.

The *Good Hope* moored at Brockweir in 1904. (Neil Parkhouse Collection)

'There is a pretty Village at Brockweir adjoining to the River upon the Forrest side, where now lying at Anchor are about 16 boats and barges, which trade to Bristol.'

Survey of the Rivers Wye and Lugg, 1697

Ferry furore

Waiting for the ferry.
(Neil Parkhouse Collection)

Brockweir ferry had been run by the Dibden family for at least three generations before a group of wealthy incomers set out plans to build a bridge across the Wye, putting the ferry business in jeopardy. In 1907 Edward Dibden, who owned the ferry and lived in the distinctive Quay House beside the wharf, resorted to the High Court to protect his livelihood.

Passengers rang a bell at the landing steps on the Welsh side to call the ferry. On the Brockweir (English) side they called at Quay House. Crossing was on demand between 7am and 10pm in the summer and 9pm in winter (except for emergencies and to fetch the doctor from Tintern).

The ferry made about £124 a year and Dibden wanted 'an injunction and damages against the disturbance of an ancient ferry across the Wye'. He lost the case and was bankrupted. The construction of the bridge signalled the end for the ancient ferry, just as the coming of the railway in 1876 killed off most of the river trade.

Like most of the villages along the Wye, Brockweir had a regular market boat to Bristol. Owned by Edward Dibden, the steamer *La Belle Marie* was the last Bristol boat operating until about 1910. The ferry is crossing far right in this picture c. 1905. (Neil Parkhouse Collection)

Above: Brockweir bridge under construction, 1906. Once connected with the Chepstow to Monmouth road the focus of life in this riverside village changed forever. (Neil Parkhouse Collection)

The ferryman at Tintern, c. 1895.
(Neil Parkhouse Collection)

'The way to enjoy Tintern Abbey properly... is to bring wines, cold meat, with corn for the horses; (bread, beer, cyder, and commonly salmon, may be had at the Beaufort Arms); spread your table in the ruins.'

John Byng, 1781

Tintern Abbey
'A most picturesque and justly celebrated ruin'

Many tourists were dismayed by the beggars and hovels surrounding Tintern Abbey. Their first view of the architectural highlight of the Wye Tour did not live up to Gilpin's description of 'the most beautiful and picturesque view on the river' – his third grand scene.

The Abbey had been a tourist destination since the 1750s when the Duke of Beaufort cleared the interior, laying a lawn to make it easier for visitors to view the ruins. But 'the ill-placed neatness...turf as even and trim as a

When the turnpike road opened in 1828 it made it easier for visitors to arrive by horse and coach. (Gloucestershire Archives)

bowling- green' annoyed many tourists including Francis Grose who, in 1772, felt it gave 'the building more of an air of an artificial ruin in a garden than that of an ancient decayed abbey'.

By the 19th century the Abbey had become a victim of its success: 'By means of steps, rails, and planks, all travellers, even elderly ladies, may safely traverse the walls of Tintern from summit to floor, a circumstance greatly extolled by many wanderers in search of the picturesque', but which Thomas Roscoe in 1839 thought to be 'a material detraction from enjoyment; such pretty arrangements and contrivances are quite out of taste with the solemn grandeur of this glorious relic'. Too many people were taking John Byng's advice to 'spread their table' and lunch in the ruins. Whilst Louisa Ann Twamley was enjoying the 'pure and beautiful symmetry' of the Abbey in 1838, one of the lunchers spoilt the 'calm, venerable and solemn character' of the place by declaring too loudly 'Where can John have put the sandwiches?'

Some of the tourists had ideas about how the visitor experience might be improved. John Byng thought that, 'At some trifling expense, the surrounding cottages and orchards might be removed' to open up the view. And not all the locals shared the tourists' appreciation of history. William Sparks, a local barge builder, attacked a statue in the Abbey severing the head from the body which was then used as a backstop for quoits!

Despite all the moans the majority felt that the Abbey was 'a most picturesque and justly celebrated ruin'. As William Makepeace Thackeray put it in 1842, 'I never saw such a magnificent elegance and simplicity in any gothic building.'

In the 1880s after the railway arrived, Tintern became a popular excursion destination. Midnight trips to view the harvest moon rising through the rose window of Tintern Abbey became fashionable.

'Thanks to the railways' one local doctor wrote, 'vast numbers now rusticate for a season amidst the recesses of Wales'. The Old Station at Tintern remains a popular destination as a visitor centre and country park.

The Angidy Valley
Cradle of industry

Although the romantic ruins of Tintern Abbey were the highlight of the Wye Tour, Tintern was also an industrial village and 'the great ironworks, which introduce noise and bustle unto these regions of tranquillity' inspired many travellers looking for the picturesque. For more than 300 years Tintern's metal industries were at the cutting edge of industrial development in Britain.

Making Britain less dependent on imported goods had been government policy during Elizabeth I's reign. The Company of Mineral and Battery Works was set up in 1566 and given a monopoly to produce wire which was a highly valuable commodity. The Company looked for suitable sites for waterwheels and found the Angidy, a gurgling brook which runs into the Wye at Tintern. Works were established here, probably on the site of what is today called the Lower Wireworks.

Needing European expertise, skilled workers were brought from Germany to Tintern. Known locally as 'strangers', they took five years to train up local men and perfect the art of 'wire drawing'. Before long Tintern men were drawing great lengths of wire from one inch cubes of iron. Marmaduke Rawdon who visited in 1665 wrote about the wire workers who 'draw wire from little iron barrs into several sieses, a curiostie worth the seeing'.

Tintern produced some of the best wire in the country and by 1600 the wireworks were the largest industrial enterprise in Wales, employing hundreds of people. Large quantities of wire were sent to workers in Bristol who made knitting needles, fishing hooks, bird cages and buckles. Wire was also used in fashionable Elizabethan clothing, whilst thousands of people were employed making wire into carding combs for the woollen industry, wool being Britain's main export at this time.

'great ironworks...introduce noise and bustle unto these regions of tranquillity'

One of the waterwheels along the Angidy, with Tintern Abbey in the distance. F. Calvert, 1815. (Chepstow Museum)

Pontysaeson Dam. A leat carried water from the storage pond here to Abbey Tintern Furnace half a mile away.

James Wathen's view of a mill in Tintern, probably the Lower Wireworks, in 1798. (Herefordshire Archive Service)

A job at the wireworks was much sought after and wireworkers became the local elite. They enjoyed voting rights, tax concessions, sick pay and pensions which were paid to those too old to work. The company funded a priest and a school teacher and supplied ale and tobacco for the annual wireworks feast. When the plague arrived in the village the company 'did relieve divers distressed and sick persons'. There was even 'a garden for the use of the people at the Furnace'.

Making wire was a skilled and time consuming activity, involving a number of different but linked processes. Hundreds of people were employed in one of the first integrated industrial complexes in the country. A constant supply of water was essential and a system of water engineering involving storage ponds, dams and leats was constructed. Where the Angidy flowed into the Wye at Abbey Mill a tidal dock was created to allow trows to load and unload even at low tide.

This industrial activity was well established by the time the Wye Tourists flocked to Tintern. They loved the sounds of the huge forge hammers hitting metal, the thick smoke which hung over the Valley and the glow in the night sky from the furnace and forges. By the nineteenth century there were twenty or more waterwheels along the Angidy and one truly massive waterwheel stood on the river bank in Tintern, described by a visitor as having 'the power of eighty horses'.

The wireworks continued until the 19th century. Local tradition has it that Angidy wire was used in the first transatlantic telegraph cable. By this time the industry was in decline: steam was replacing waterpower and the rushing water of the Angidy no longer held an advantage. In 1878 a new company began manufacturing tinplate but by 1895 the local newspaper was reporting that, 'Tintern Tin Works, which have been going irregularly for some time past, closed up last Sunday with no hope of an immediate restart.' With the closure of the works 350 years of metal working in the Angidy came to an end. In the 20th century the site became a saw mill for stone and later timber.

The only waterwheel to survive today is at Abbey Mill, whilst the most visible evidence of the Valley's former industry is the Wireworks Bridge, built across the Wye in 1876 to link the wireworks with the railway network. Ironically, by this time, the works were in decline and the bridge never really fulfilled its function.

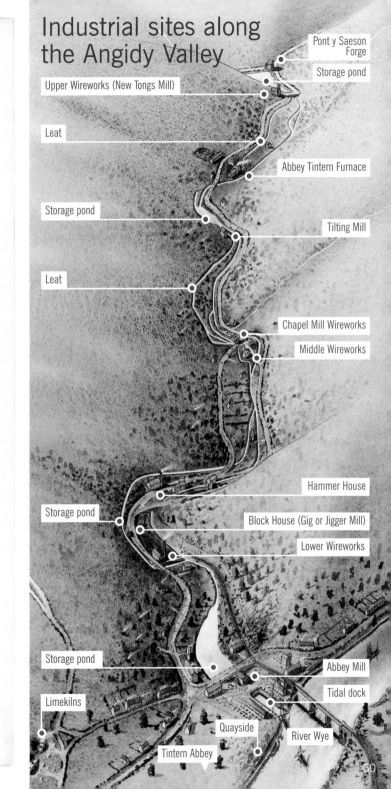

Industrial sites along the Angidy Valley

Pont y Saeson Forge

Storage pond

Upper Wireworks (New Tongs Mill)

Leat

Abbey Tintern Furnace

Storage pond

Tilting Mill

Leat

Chapel Mill Wireworks

Middle Wireworks

Hammer House

Storage pond

Block House (Gig or Jigger Mill)

Lower Wireworks

Storage pond

Abbey Mill

Tidal dock

Limekilns

Quayside

River Wye

Tintern Abbey

The riverside was a bustling place, with boats, a bark store and the Quay Master's house. Tanner's ships would have moored here, or at the tidal dock at Abbey Mill, to unload iron ore and load finished iron products like cannons! Detail from *Tintern Abbey*, John Varley, 1832. (Chepstow Museum)

Large warehouses stand beside the tidal dock at Abbey Mill, and a trow is moored downstream of the Wireworks Bridge, c. 1885. (Neil Parkhouse Collection)

Abbey Tintern Furnace
'A noble foundary of cannon'

Abbey Tintern Furnace was built by Thomas Foley in 1672-3 to produce a special type of iron – osmond iron – needed by the wireworks. A century later a visitor to Tintern found a 'noble foundary of cannon' at the furnace. Ironmaster David Tanner was making cannons to supply the British forces fighting in the American War of Independence. Tanner was one of the most important ironmasters in Wales in the late 1700s. He was in business in a big way, owning the furnace, forges and wireworks along the Angidy between 1772 and 1798, leasing forges across Monmouthshire and owning ships to transport iron ore from Lancashire to his furnaces.

Demand for cannon rocketed during Britain's fight to retain its colonies in America. At this time Britain's battle ships could have 40 or 50 cannon on board. Ironmasters like David Tanner were under pressure to deliver, but his

> ## 'A Continual Din of Hammers is to be heard here a very Considerable Iron Work being carried on by a Mr Tanner.'
> Francis Grose, 1775

How Abbey Tintern Furnace may have looked around 1780 when David Tanner was producing cannons. (Illustration by Phil Kenning)

cannons rarely passed the government's strict new quality controls, which specified that guns must be cast solid. This meant cutting moulds into the ground, up to 9 feet deep, pouring the molten iron in and then boring out the centre. Few iron makers had experience of this technique. Tanner sent his cannons to the Woolwich Arsenal where a master gun founder checked quality. In 1783 he was caught concealing defects in his guns (using black paint), an unforgiveable act in time of war.

Tanner's enemies tried to bankrupt him and he spent a year in prison, until the case against him was withdrawn. Had it been proved it would have been the biggest bankruptcy ever seen outside London at that time. His Tintern properties were sold in 1798 and he was last heard of on a boat bound for Bengal. He left behind a large industrial operation at Tintern – one of the first integrated industrial complexes in the country. 'To his spirit the works at Tintern are indebted for their improvements' wrote Charles Heath in 1801, 'as well as the trade at its present extensive connections.'

Tanner's guns were always cast with a large 'T' on them for Tintern or Tanner. Some failed government quality controls and were shipped to Istanbul! (Fort Amherst)

The Vale of Tintern from the Devil's Pulpit, W. H. Bartlett, 1845.

Offa's Dyke
King Offa's 'keep out' sign?

This is border country and the remains of an impressive bank and ditch, which once defined much of the boundary between what we now call England and Wales, runs south of Monmouth on high ground looking over the river towards Wales. This ancient earthwork was built by Offa, ruler of the Anglo-Saxon kingdom of Mercia from 757 - 796 AD. Offa's Dyke would have been a symbol of his power and authority as well as a formidable obstacle to any invaders. It was designed to impress, with the surrounding trees cleared to ensure the dyke was highly visible in the landscape.

As Britain's longest ancient monument Offa's Dyke has had a lasting impact on the way people living either side of it define their cultural identity. It certainly intrigued the Wye Tourists. Thomas Roscoe described how, 'an ancient entrenchment runs some distance along the ridge of the hill, and one angle, commanding a splendid view of Tintern and the fair vale around it, is dignified by the appellation of the "Devil's Pulpit".' This is a narrow pillar of limestone on the edge of the Wye gorge providing a bird's eye view over Tintern Abbey. Legend has it that the Devil used to preach from the 'pulpit' trying to seduce the Abbey's monks to join him! Now on the route of the Offa's Dyke Path National Trail, the Devil's Pulpit remains a popular viewpoint.

'The guides or boatmen will point attention to Plumber's Cliff, which is surmounted by an ancient intrenchment, the highest point of which is the Devil's Pulpit'.

The Halls, 1861

An artist's impression of how Offa's Dyke may have looked in the landscape some 1200 years ago. (Alan Duncan)

Outdoor service at Lancaut in the 1930s. (Neil Parkhouse Collection)

Lancaut, c. 1900.

Lancaut
Splendid isolation

Enclosed within a sweeping bend of the River Wye and bordered by steep limestone cliffs, Lancaut is, quite literally, a lost place.
The ruins of St James Church are all that remain of a medieval village, a silent reminder that for centuries people farmed, fished and worshipped here.

The tiny church is of Celtic origin. A monastery was recorded here in 703 and the name Lancaut is probably an English corruption of the Welsh *Llan* for church and *Cewydd*, a 6th century Welsh saint. When Offa's Dyke was built in the 8th century an Iron Age hillfort at Spital Meend (above Lancaut) was incorporated into Offa's ditch and bank defences. As the Dyke passed to the east of Lancaut the church remained under Welsh control (despite being on the wrong side of the river) until the 10th century. Lancaut may have been linked to the Cistercian monks who founded Tintern Abbey in 1131. It has been rebuilt on several occasions since the late 12th century.

We don't know why the village died. Perhaps life on this isolated promontory became too much of a struggle. As the number of villagers declined so did the services in the church and from the 1750s only twelve services a year were held. But the church remained a 'favourite resort' well into the 19th century and Eleanor Ormerod described how the congregation were 'packed as tightly as could be managed, so that we all had to get up and sit down together'. Eleanor's father George Ormerod was a local antiquary who recorded details of the church in the 1840s and 50s. In 1865 the church was finally abandoned.

Trows loading at Lancaut. (Chepstow Museum)

Riches in the cliffs

The towering cliffs surrounding Lancaut have been quarried for centuries for their limestone.
Just a stone's throw from the church stood jetties where the trows were loaded. The *Ringdove*, *Squirrel*, *Sampson*, *Wye* and the *George and Mary* were just some of the vessels that carried limestone to build new docks at Avonmouth in the 1870s. The *Spry*, and the *Nelly* took limestone to Newport and Cardiff to build docks there too. Between the two World Wars the *Palace*, worked by Captain Sims and his sons, carried Lancaut stone to sites along the Severn where the sea defences were being strengthened. Many local men worked these quarries until they closed in the 1950s.

Picturesque Piercefield
'The most pleasing riot of imagination'

Lying just across the river from Lancaut was Piercefield, the highlight at the end of the Wye Tour. This estate looks out over a great loop in the river Wye, stretching from the Wyndcliff down to Chepstow. When Valentine Morris inherited Piercefield in 1743 he set about creating a landscape on a truly grand scale. Laying out paths and clearing trees, he constructed grottos and follies and romantically named viewpoints such as the Lover's Leap, Double View and The Giant's Cave. The result was one of the most outstanding examples of 18th century picturesque landscaping in Britain. 'Mr Morris's improvements at Persfield' wrote Gilpin, 'are generally thought as much worth a traveller's notice, as anything on the banks of the Wye.' And although Gilpin didn't feel that the views were properly picturesque he did think

they were 'extremely romantic, and give a loose to the most pleasing riot of imagination'.

In the 18th century most tourists alighted from their boats at Martridge Meadow. 'The tide being at ebb, we landed with some difficulty on an oozy beach,' wrote William Gilpin. 'One of our bargemen, who knew the place, served as a guide; and under his conduct we climbed the steep by an easy regular zig-zag.' Their goal was the Wyndcliff, 'the last grand scene of the Piercefield drama. It is not only magnificent, but so novel, that it excites an involuntary start of astonishment; and so sublime, that it elevates the mind into instantaneous rapture'. This was the highest point on the Piercefield Walks with a view which Coleridge described as 'the whole world imaged in its vast circumference'.

The new turnpike road built through the lower Wye Valley in the 1820s made it easier for visitors to arrive by carriage. A 'fanciful little habitation, called the Moss Cottage' was built beside the new road by the Duke of Beaufort to

'Let the reader imagine a continuous 'range' of walks, of more than three miles in extent, laid out with consummate skill'

The Halls, 1861

View from the Alcove, Ralph Lucas.
(Chepstow Museum)

'a pretty little toy of a cottage... all daintily covered in moss', wrote Thackeray in 1842. The original Moss Cottage was demolished in the 1950s. (Chepstow Museum)

provide refreshments for the growing number of visitors, who increased dramatically following the introduction of regular steam packet services from Bristol to Chepstow. The Duke made other enhancements including the Eagle's Nest, a double decker viewing platform perched on the summit of the Wyndcliff, linked to Moss Cottage via three hundred and sixty-five steps. It was 'A curious descent ... by means of ingenious zig-zag walks and rude steps down which a guide leads you,' wrote William Makepeace Thackeray in 1842. When the Halls toured in 1861 they had to pay sixpence: 'The fee is designed to effect what it does effect – a barrier to prevent the intrusions of mere idlers from the town, who would disturb the tranquillity of the scene'!

The Giant's Cave was a favourite with visitors who were advised to 'Carry some gunpowder and leave it with Mr Morris's gardener in order to fire some small cannon on the Rock as you pass by. The reverberating echo of which you will find has a wonderful effect.' At one time a stone

View from the Wyndcliffe, Ralph Lucas.
(Chepstow Museum)

The Lion's Lodge. (Chepstow Museum)

giant stood above the cave entrance. He held a huge boulder over his head, as if about to hurl it on the walkers below. The giant and his boulder suffered from frost damage and slowly crumbled away. Further along the path was the Lover's Leap and 'In a charming and sequestered spot ... a cold bath supplied by a copious and transparent rill, which springs at the foot of the winding cliff, and ripples down the side of the declivity.'

Later owners of Piercefield made the Lion's Lodge (south of the racecourse) the main entrance. Arriving at the Lodge in 1838 Louisa Anne Twamley described meeting 'a small boy, who walked with us to a tall tree, and catching at a rope hanging from it, rang such a sonorous peal on a great bell hidden among the branches....This startling summons... brought the guide to our assistance, we were conducted to the Alcove, the first view-point, and then in succession to the eight others.'

Not everyone shared the Piercefield mania. Thomas Roscoe thought that 'Grottos fabricated where grottos

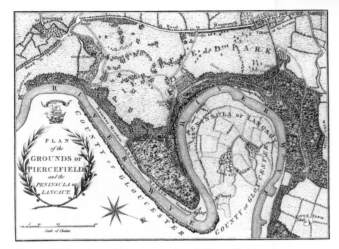

Above: This plan of the grounds of Piercefield and the Lancaut peninsula comes from William Coxe's *Historical Tour in Monmouthshire, 1801*. (Chepstow Museum) Below: Detail from Piercefield Mansion and Park, c. 1840, G. Eyre Brooks. (Chepstow Museum)

could not naturally exist, with dilapidated giants in stone over their entrance and inscriptions, not of the highest order of composition, are very well calculated to make the unlearned stare, as sure as to make the judicious grieve'.

Piercefield House dates from after Valentine Morris's death, when Sir John Soane was commissioned to redesign it. A curving portico and flanking pavilions by Joseph Bonomi were added later. The history of Piercefield is intertwined with the slave trade. Valentine Morris was the son of a wealthy sugar plantation owner from Antigua. When he owned Piercefield he also owned slaves named Piercefield, Beaufort and Chepstow. Nathaniel Wells, the son of another plantation owner and a black slave, bought Piercefield in 1802. He was sent to Britain to be educated and became a respected member of Monmouthshire society, a magistrate and in 1818 High Sheriff.

Today Piercefield is a Grade 1 Registered Historic Park and Garden and the house is listed. Some of the vistas which surprised and charmed earlier visitors have been lost, but enough of Valentine's viewpoints remain to take your breath away.

The view from the house is soft, rich, and beautifully picturesque...an elegant arrangement of lawn, wood, and water.'

The Times, 1798

'*So uncommonly excellent, that the most exact critic in landscape would scarcely wish to alter a position in the assemblage of woods, cliffs, ruins and water.*'

Wyndham, 1774

Tourists passing under the bridge at Chepstow at the end of the Wye Tour, 1826. (Chepstow Museum)

Chepstow
Port, pleasure boats and packets

Chepstow, controlling the mouth of the Wye, had been an important port since at least the Middle Ages.
A huge tidal range allowed sea-going ships to sail up to Chepstow. The Norman Lords along the border with Wales paid no customs to the Crown, in return for defending and extending English territory, so that during this period Chepstow was a free port. Wine imported here was duty-free and could be re-shipped to Bristol to avoid customs. With such a competitive advantage trade flourished. Imports of wine came from Spain, Gascony and Portugal and stockfish and salt came from Iceland. It wasn't until 1573 that a customs house was established in the town and the duty-free privileges were lost. Despite foreign trade

declining, the river trade prospered, particularly as industries developed along the Wye in the 17th and 18th centuries.

Chepstow was the largest port in South Wales when it became a bonded port in 1838. Vast quantities of timber and bark were exported. The river trade and its associated activities – ship building, timber yards, warehouses, saw mills, rope works and brickyards – stretched from above the Wye Bridge right down to the cliffs at Bulwark. Gunstock Wharf was the heart of the port, where a dry dock could repair ships of 500 tons. Surrounding the dock were warehouses, some built partly of slag blocks from the up-river industries. The market trows for Bristol left from the adjacent Packet Slip. Press gangs would have operated in The Back, a densely packed area of warehouses and inns south of the dock.

The *Wye* steamer passing under Brunel's bridge enroute for Bristol. Timber is stacked up on the left bank, close to the site of the bonded timber yard. (Chepstow Museum)

The *War Glory* leaving Chepstow following her launch in 1920.

Below Brunel's railway bridge across the Wye was Finch's ship yard. Edward Finch had come to Chepstow to construct the railway bridge in 1846. He stayed in the town, establishing a shipyard which also built iron ship masts, bridges and dock gates. This site became the Standard Ship Building Company during WW1, and was taken over by the government in 1917 to form National Shipyard No 1. Eight slipways were constructed to build merchant ships to replace those being lost to U-boats. In the 1920s the ship yards were acquired by Fairfield, which as Mabey Bridge continue Chepstow's bridge building tradition to this day.

Trade through Chepstow declined towards the end of the 19th century. When the customs house closed in 1882 it signalled that for Chepstow attention was shifting to the rapidly growing coal ports of South Wales.

The arrival of the first steam packet boat in Chepstow in 1822 changed the Wye Tour forever. The daily services between Bristol and Chepstow by the *Duke of Beaufort* and the *Wye* opened up the Wye Valley to the residents of Bristol. A bell now rang to signal arrivals and departures at the Packet Slip and before long the day trippers outnumbered the traditional tourists who arrived by tour boat from Ross. 'Our solitude was invaded by a cargo of passengers, landed at Chepstow from on board the Bristol steam-boat, who rushed in with sketch-books, eye-glasses, parasols, best bonnets, McIntosh cloaks, baskets of provisions, and every sort of luxury considered essential to the full enjoyment of beautiful scenery or ruined abbeys' complained Catherine Sinclair in her diary of 1833.

As Chepstow's importance as a centre for tourism increased townhouses near the river were converted into hotels, including the Chepstow Castle Inn and the Castle View Hotel. The town was well placed for the day trippers who wanted to see Piercefield and Tintern Abbey. 'The excursion from Chepstow to Tintern is of the exact length and comfort to suit a Londoner's taste,' wrote Thackeray in 1842. 'A fly, at a moderate remuneration, will 'waft you'... from the old town to the old abbey, and restore you to your inn in four hours, of which not one minute has been tedious.' What better recommendation could you have for a visit to the Wye Valley?

The scale of National Shipyard Number 1 dwarfed Brunel's bridge over the Wye, c. 1919.

Overlooking the Wye

Dros Ddyffryn Gwy

Between 2008 and 2012 the Overlooking the Wye Landscape Partnership Scheme invested £3m into the local economy. Over 40 sites, including all the ones featured in this book, benefited from conservation, access or interpretation work. As many structures had fallen into a serious state of disrepair and were becoming unsafe, the Overlooking the Wye Scheme proved very timely in saving these special places for future generations. Work ranged from archaeological digs, through extensive rebuilding and repointing of masonry structures, to pathway improvements and the installation of artwork. Over 14,000 people enjoyed a varied programme of walks, talks and training activities as well as attending events which celebrated the history of the Wye Valley. Plaques and panels explaining the history of each site now help visitors understand and appreciate their significance.

Conservation work was a highly specialised task. Most of the viewpoints are perched precariously on the edges of cliffs overlooking the valley, whilst the riverside quays and industrial sites are regularly inundated by tides or floods. Many sites are Scheduled Monuments and the river and much of the woodland in the Wye Valley are also internationally important for nature conservation as well as being in an Area of Outstanding Natural Beauty (AONB). Conservation work had to be planned and undertaken with sensitivity to these challenges and constraints. Completed with considerable difficulty today, the conservation work illustrates the complex issues which had to be overcome when these sites were originally constructed some 250 years ago. So when you stand and stare - overlooking the Wye - spare a thought for those who originally made it possible.

Top left: Elements of historic wire making at Tintern were depicted by local ceramics artist Ned Heywood. He created a variety of interpretative artworks and plaques at sites ranging from the remote Lancaut church, to Coppet Hill limekilns and the port of Chepstow. He also worked with art students from Chepstow Comprehensive to create a mural at Abbey Mill in Tintern. Top right: Overlooking the Wye from Eagle's Nest.

We would like to thank our partners and funders

£1.9 million from the Heritage Lottery Fund was matched with £100,000 of volunteer support and £1 million of contributions from the following partners:

adventa, Bridstow Parish Council, Cadw, Chepstow Town Council, Coppett Hill Common Trust, Countryside Council for Wales (CCW), CPRW, Dean Local Action, English Bicknor Parish Council, English Heritage, Forest of Dean District Council, Forestry Commission (England), Forestry Commission (Wales), Friends of Coppett Hill, Gloucestershire County Council, Gloucestershire Environmental Trust, Herefordshire Council, Hewelsfield & Brockweir Parish Council, Lydbrook Parish Council, Mabey Bridge, Monmouth Town Council, Monmouthshire County Council, National Grid, National Trust, Natural England, PRISM, private landowners, Ross Civic Society, Ross Town Council, Sustainable Development Fund (SDF) (England & Wales), Tintern Community Council, Trellech United Community Council, Woodland Trust, Wye Valley AONB Partnership, Wye Valley Centre (Abbey Mill, Tintern), Wynndel Property Management.

Overlooking the Wye would not have been such a success without the guidance of the Partnership Board, chaired by Cllr Phil Cutter, the dedication of the Implementation Team: Sue Middleton, Kate Biggs, Julie Godfrey and Ruth Waycott, and the support of the Wye Valley AONB Unit: Andrew Blake, Andrew Nixon, Sarah Sawyer, Nikki Moore & Sharon Seymour.

For three summers Monmouth Comprehensive School Year 7 pupils spent days out discovering their local heritage through the Scheme. Over 1,000 pupils took part and education packs are available from www.wyevalleyaonb.org.uk for others to follow in their footsteps.

Working between the tides, Sally Strachey Conservation carefully rebuilt and repointed Brockweir and Monmouth quays. Throughout the scheme project management, engineering and safety work was overseen by Opus International.

Rope access and conservation specialists, Ascend, repaired six 18th century viewpoints on the Piercefield estate; some were on the verge of collapsing into the river. They also worked on Abbey Tintern Furnace, Lower Wireworks, New Weir Forge and Whitecliff Furnace, near Coleford, often abseiling down with buckets of mortar. During Overlooking the Wye they employed and trained three new staff in heritage conservation skills.

A map of the river Wye and adjacent country from Ross to Chepstow, c. 1845.

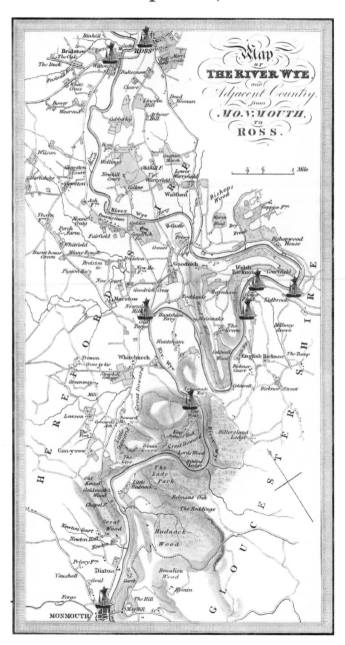

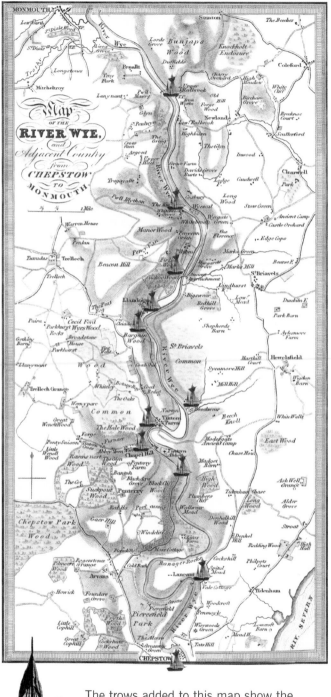

The trows added to this map show the location of wharves along the Wye.